AUTHOR ALIX STRAUSS FOUND OUT BRITNEY'S FAVORITES—

AND YOU CAN TOO:

- Favorite color: baby blue
- Favorite actor: Tom Cruise
- Favorite store: The Gap
- Favorite designer: Betsey Johnson
- Favorite ice cream flavor: cookie dough
- Favorite movie: *My Best Friend's Wedding*

Britney Spears

Alix Strauss

St. Martin's Paperbacks

BRITNEY SPEARS

Copyright © 1999 by Alix Strauss.
Cover photograph © Eddie Malluk/Retna.

ISBN: 0-312-97268-7

Printed in the United States of America

St. Martin's Paperbacks edition/August 1999

10 9 8 7

For Britney's Friends, Family, and of course, her Fans

Acknowledgments

Many thanks to the following people whose help and time have been instrumental in making this book come together: My agent, Giles Anderson, for his witty conversation; my editor, Joe Veltre, for his kindness and faith; and Amy Maclin for her keen eye and sense of humor.

Table of Contents

Britney 101

In the Beginning

We open in a small, friendly town in Kentwood, Louisiana. Here, apple pie is actually baked fresh in the A.M. and left out to cool by an open window. There's no smog, no dirty garbage or empty soda cans strewn all over the street, no barking horns from frustrated drivers—just a mellow sort of bliss.

A little girl of three years old is dancing around the living room, acting out groovy songs and singing into a hairspray bottle, a suitable stand-in for a mike. In another part of the ranch-style house, a mom is going batty hearing her daughter perform the song for the umpteenth time. But in all honesty, she doesn't really mind. The girl, of course, is Britney Spears, and by the time she reaches the ripe old age of 16, almost everyone will know her name, her voice, and her music.

"I drove my mom crazy, but she got used to

it,'' Britney shares in *Girl's Life*. ''One day I was jumping on my trampoline singing, and my mom realized I could carry a tune. I think that's when I first thought about going into entertainment.''

Her mom, Lynn, a second-grade schoolteacher, was pleasantly surprised. According to Britney, the only other artistic person in their family is someone who plays an instrument on her mother's side—not a good sign. Still, no one thought much about the incident. No one could have guessed what lay ahead, or what would happen over the next decade. Not her parents, older brother, younger sister, or even Britney.

An Original

Aside from having a memory for songs and an inner, almost inherent, connection to music, as a child Britney had a personal desire and a big dream. She wanted to be a pop star.

She had her heroes picked out early on. Mariah Carey, Whitney Houston, and Prince were her team captains. She sang their songs, practiced and copied their voices, and taught herself their dance steps. The singing bug had bitten Britney hard. She was consumed by music. She put her vocal cords to work by singing in school plays, in recitals, in talent shows, the shower, while walking to school, while coming home from school . . .

anywhere possible. At age four she gave her first public appearance. At seven she took gymnastics and dance classes, and before age ten she was on national TV. As if she were preparing for her future, Britney seemed to be in a constant state of rehearsal.

Because of all of her early accomplishments, super sound, and hip dance tunes, Britney's been compared to some of the most successful artists and commercial vocalists today: Alanis Morrissette, Tiffany (anyone remember her?), Toni Braxton, and the Spice Girls to name a few, but don't be so quick to pigeonhole her. Even Debbie Gibson would be slightly jealous. The two, however, are not synonymous. Aside from their young age and that they both sing pop songs, "our music is totally different," Britney tells one interviewer. "I'm a lot edgier." Lucky for us, Britney's totally original and impressively unique.

Home Sweet Home

Located off the cuff of Louisiana, teetering on the edge of the Mississippi border, you'll find Kentwood, a charming, small community where everyone knows everyone, and all are like family. Britney grew up in a rural town, very much like Laura Ingalls did on *Little House on the Prairie*. Okay, obviously it's more modern than that, but not by much. Kentwood is really small. How small is it? It's so small that has only two main streets. It's so tiny that the town has a few grocery stores, a post office, a furniture shop and a funeral home—that's all. It's so very little that only 2,400 people live there. That's almost the amount of people it takes just to keep Madonna happy. "Everyone is like family," explains Darlene Hughes, Britney's third-grade teacher. Not only does Mrs. Hughes still educate at Park Lane School, Britney's old stomping ground, but she also spreads glowing reports and updates the kids about her little prodigy, just like a proud parent. "There are lot of dairy farmers and churchgoers; everyone sticks together." A tight group composed of neighbors and friends—it's not Mulberry Street, but it's the closest thing to it.

Britney is a giver of sorts, to her family, her fans, even to her hometown. "I like having people hear my music," she says to *Pop* magazine. "If I can entertain them and bring them some pleasure, that's the greatest satisfaction that I can have." In fact, Britney helped put Kentwood on the map. It's become as famous as she is—well, almost. MTV, VH-1, and *Rolling Stone* have all made appearances at her school. Endless articles, interviews, and radio shows have all mentioned where Britney grew up. In return, Kentwood has given something back to the superstar in appreciation, an official Britney Spears Day. How cool is that? Having a whole village celebrate your special day. Talk about being king of the world— well, maybe that's queen. "The town celebrates her birthday at the ball field," Mrs. Hughes says, "There's a banner that hangs over the road when you get off the interstate." It reads proudly "HOME OF OUR STAR, BRITNEY SPEARS."

Family Matters

You don't need to know them personally to see how family-oriented and close the Spears are.

Britney comes from a very supportive home—any more wholesome and you'd confuse them with the Cleavers or a smaller version of *7th Heaven*, before the birth of the twins. Dad's a contractor, Mom's a second-grade teacher. They have three kids, all well adjusted, sweet, and happy. Bryan, who's 21, is five years older than Britney, and Jamie Lynn (her name is a combination of both her parents' first names) who just turned eight, is nine years younger than her sis. Britney may be a middle child, but she's no Jan Brady. "Britney and Bryan take after their dad in the looks department," says one family friend. "Her sister, Jamie Lynn, has more of her mom's coloring." They have three dogs, probably some fish, maybe a bird, and, chances are, a sign which reads "HOME SWEET HOME" hanging somewhere in the kitchen. But Britney says, like most families, they can drive her crazy. Still, as you could guess, her family are her biggest fans. How big? Well, many years ago, the Spears' living room mantle was stacked with Britney's prizes from pageants, talent shows, and gymnastics competitions. There's even a big silver trophy for winning the Miss Talent USA pageant in Monroe, Louisiana. It resides on the floor because, at 58 inches, it's probably taller than young Britney was when she won it. Now the family's mantel is full of picture frames with newspaper clippings, press releases, and photo ops with big-name stars.

* * *

Not everyone thought the Spears should have let Britney travel so far away at such a young age. Many people from her hometown were concerned, and thought the Spears might be making the wrong choice, sending their little girl out into the cruel, crazy world of music. But Britney is living proof her parents made the right decision, and in turn, she gives them a lot of credit. Not only was it a difficult choice to make, and a family-altering judgment that would affect everyone involved, but it was hard to know if they were actually doing the right thing. "It was unheard of," Britney admits in an article. "I come from a really, really small town and they were like, 'You're sending your daughter to New York? Are you crazy?'" But worry not. Britney has a trustworthy adult, Felicia Culotta, a family friend who travels with her and keeps a watchful eye. "They made such a great effort to keep life as normal for her as possible," reports Mrs. Hughes. "Her parents were always very supportive." Mom helped make sure Britney kept up with her schoolwork. Mrs. Hughes would fax lesson plans, homework, and tests to her while she was working in New York.

Luckily, Lynn's no stage mother or Mommy Dearest. On the contrary, she's totally the opposite. Still, that doesn't stop her from being concerned. After all, worrying is in a mother's job description. "I worry about her terribly," her mom admits to *People* magazine. "But I'm so much happier knowing she's doing what she really wants."

Ironically, Britney is the real driving force behind the idea. "Most parents are the one pushing the child. I was the one who wanted it," Britney confides to AOL's Entertainment Asylum. "I'm thankful because they were so supportive." They truly went the extra mile that most parents don't always go. They let Britney make some mighty large decisions but had enough faith in her and believed that this was something she had to do, a calling she needed to fulfill. There is an enormous amount of passion required to take hold of what you want. Britney had family endorsement, desire, and drive, but most important, she had belief in herself and in her talent.

There were a few times, however, when Britney thought her ambitions and desires for a singing career were just a fantasy. Who was she kidding? Everyone dreams of becoming rich and famous. Everyone wants to be a superstar. And everyone wants to make a record and become a pop sensation. But she'd shake that voice out of her head, the one that said, "You can't, you're not good enough, it's just a dream" and replaced it with "You've got to go for it. You've got to try. You go girl."

Because Britney seemed so hard on herself, her parents didn't need to put any additional pressure on her. Rather, she put enough on herself for everyone. "When I was younger, I would cry if I missed gymnastics," says Britney, "and my mom was always like, 'Brinnie, are you sure this is what you want?' " She'd dry her eyes and nod that she did. And like a champ, she'd make sure she was ready next time.

Lynn might be Britney's biggest fan, but the feeling is mutual. "My mom is so sweet," says Britney in a *Girl's Life* interview. "She helped me become who I am, and she taught me to have strength." The two talk daily. Mom visits a lot, and when possible, Jamie Lynn comes along for the ride.

Brother Bryan, who is at college majoring in kinesiology, the study of how mechanics and anatomy make the human body move—ugh! that sounds hard—at Southeastern Louisiana University, remembers Britney having an ache for acting and drama early on. "She would put on makeup," he tells an interviewer, "and sing to herself in the bathroom mirror." Bryan recalls his kid sister as being "basically a pain." Not a surprising or an uncommon answer coming from an older bro.

Britney, of course, remembers it being the other way around. "*He* was the pain," she claims, contradicting his comment, in a recent interview. "He's like the overprotective brother, which is good. You want that in an older brother." He too seems totally comfortable with his kid sister out in the real world doing her singing thing. Though he is often caught playing the fatherly role, always looking out for his kid sister. "When I come home it's different," she assures *MTV News*. "Like he trusts me out 'cause he can't do anything about it. So when I come home, he's like, 'Where are you going? What are you doing?'" As if Kentwood were more dangerous than New York? Like Britney could get into more trouble there! Bryan has also been quoted as claiming to have taught Britney everything she knows. Yeah, right. Let's reverse that one. "My brother is such a country boy," she says during an interview. Britney probably taught him all *he* knows.

Youngest on the Spears' family tree is Jamie Lynn. What does she think about her big sister's blast into stardom? She thinks it's totally cool. In fact, she can be found running around singing her older sister's songs. She even sang the same number as Britney did in her church show. Jamie Lynn's friends think Britney's cool, too. They get a little starstruck when they see Britney. "When my sister's little friends are over, it's so weird because they'll see me and come and give me a really big hug, and they're, like, staring at me. It's kinda funny."

Being in the spotlight hasn't affected Britney or given her a swelled head. Even though Britney is a pretty famous pop singer, she doesn't consider herself one. In fact, meeting famous people is what makes her most nervous. "When I meet famous people I get so star-struck I can't say anything to them," she confides to AOL online. "One time I saw Ashley Judd after I had just seen *Kiss The Girls*. My friend started talking to her, and I just stood there like an idiot. It's scary to meet someone, because you might be disappointed." No one would be displeased when meeting Britney. Part of her balance and grounding comes from her friends and family. When she comes home, to them she's just a Louisiana girl. "We love her and everything," says Robbey, a 16-year-old junior who went to school with Britney. "But when she's here, she's just Britney Spears, not 'Britney Spears "... Baby One More Time." ' " It's as if time has stood still and nothing much has changed. "My friends are like my sisters." Since she's known them all her life and has grown up with them, when she's home, life is rather normal. She doesn't worry about them treating her any differently. And they never do. She's close to all her cousins too, especially her best friend and cousin, Laura Lynn. "In friendship I look for someone you can really trust and who is really honest with you and can tell you the truth even if you don't want to hear it. Someone who is a lot like you who can laugh and [you can] have fun together. I have a lot of friends like that," she tells AOL. Her aunt also plays two kinds of roles. She's not just a relative, she's the president of The Britney Spears Fan Club, that she runs that out of her home. Even Grandma gets in on the family thing by living close and visiting often. (FYI: She owns a seafood shop that sells all sorts of fresh fish.) The Spears are really a close knit group.

Her small town and close family relationships have helped to keep Britney grounded. Her family has instilled good values, and she's got a strong head and a lot of ambition. "I know what I want out of life," she tells an interviewer over Christmas, having taken a break from touring with 'N Sync. "My morals are really strong and I have major beliefs and I think that has helped me." Her mom looks at this experience in a positive light as well. "There's a lot of kids that this would ruin, but I feel sure that this will make an even better person out of Britney," says Lynn to a reporter. "Britney could win the Academy Award in three different movies and she would still have a humble spirit."

"Britney was always very sweet," says Amy Miller, secretary at Britney's old elementary school, who used to fax Britney her homework while she was in New York. "The Spears have always been a nice family."

Britney's family and fans are not the only ones beaming with praise of her accomplishments. The entertainment industry is also stunned by the pop star, too. The reviews from writers and the press are just glowing. "Britney could fill Ginger's shoes as Normal Spice," writes Amy Sciarretto, in a recent review of the artist and her music. "You don't have to worry about Britney stealing your boyfriend. You can eat ice cream and cake with her. You can wear a green mud mask on a Friday night with her." And that's so true. In fact, that's one major quality that helps make her so real and likable. When she hurt her knee and couldn't make the Grammy's, MTV threw her a slumber party. A bunch of her friends hung out, did girly stuff, and had a grand old time. Though there was no freezing of bras, they did discuss music and the nominees.

3

School Daze

Darlene," Britney's mom told her daughter's third-grade teacher one afternoon, "we found out Brinnie can sing." That was all it took for word to get around. And in a small town, word spreads fast. "It was common knowledge that she had a talent that others didn't possess," confirms Mrs. Hughes.

Her school years were spent at the Lane Academy in Mississippi, where Britney, as her teacher puts it, was a model student. "She did her homework, never made a C, studied, and did everything a teacher wants a child to do," Mrs. Hughes says reflecting back to Britney's early days. "I still have her workbooks. I held on to every little thing she did." This includes notebooks, cards, letters, even a party gift Britney gave her daughter. "I knew she would be something special. She had a future."

She's not the only one to hold on to Britney's early Jane Hancock. Some of her classmates did the same. "She once wrote me a letter when we were in the fourth grade. It said "Please hand me your Christmas JC Penney catalog . . . I want to order a teddy bear," says Robbey. "She had just started getting famous, and for some reason I kept the letter. A few months before her song came out I found it." Good thing she didn't toss it. A lot of fans would love to have it. Just goes to show you, next time you're cleaning your closet and you come across an old love note or letter, you might think twice about throwing it out. You never know when a classmate will turn into a famous-mate.

On many special occasions Britney would be asked to sing. She performed a lot of Patsy Cline, imitating such songs as "Cry" and "Harvest Moon." Even though Britney knew she had something special she tried to blend in with the other students. "She never had a big head or showed off," assures Mrs. Hughes. Her classmates knew she had talent, too, and would often fight over her, each trying to get Britney to play with them. "She would come crying to me and say 'I want to play with everyone,' " Mrs. Hughes continues. "She wanted to be everybody's friend." Even at nine Britney was hip, cool, and a little ahead of her time.

Britney had so much natural talent that some folks were skeptical at first. After all, how could a little child of eight or nine sing so well? "People thought she was lip-synching or pantomiming, but she wasn't. People couldn't believe it was actually her, but of course it was. She could belt it out," Mrs. Hughes recalls.

Along with singing, Britney also enjoyed co-ordinating group activities and mini-shows. "She was really into gymnastics," recalls Robbey. "There were several times when she and her cousin, Erin, formed these little dancing clubs with five or so kids. They'd teach them a couple of routines, without music, and then perform the shows for us at recess." But the shows were put on hold because feelings would get hurt. Perhaps Britney will try her hand at directing—after she's done conquering the music world. Clearly, singing wasn't the only thing Britney excelled in. She loved basketball and played it like a pro. At school she was an honor student. Aside from the talent contests, she took home numerous awards and nominations in school. In the third grade she was up for the VIP Award. One year she was Homeroom Class Officer. In the ninth grade she was elected Class Beauty and won the title of Homecoming Maid.

High school wouldn't be high school without an embarrassing story or two, or three, or four. . . . Like most kids, Britney has her share of funny tales, the ones that make you cringe when some-one resurrects your past. One time she was at a track meet, all lined up and ready to run with the other girls. Everyone was in her starting position, all pumped up and set to go. And then, before Britney knew what had happened, all the girls took off. The gun was fired and off everyone went. Everyone, that is, except Britney, who says she didn't hear the shot. Another story deals with a wet orthodontic appliance. "She was to sing the National Anthem for Grandparents' Day," Mrs. Hughes remembers fondly, "and she got up to the mike, then came back over to me and shoved her retainer into my hand. And I thought, 'Wow, this kid really feels comfortable with me. So I held her retainer while she sang.' " And who can forget the famous school fountain incident? The details are a little unclear except that Britney ended up in it, wet, miserable, and totally embarrassed. Sometimes you *can* rewrite the past. When *Rolling Stone* came to her school to do a photo shoot, you can bet there was no wet singer. And I'm sure Britney stayed clear of that fountain, too.

4

Building a Résumé

Finding My Religion

Cute, bubbly, and talented, Britney showed signs of success early on. Her first public performance was at her church. She was only four years old and sang "What Child Is This," (rumor has it there's a videotape floating around of her crooning this little ditty).

She performed at dance recitals and blew kisses at the audience. It seems she knew the steps and how to charm a crowd even at three. When she was five, her song won first place in the Kentwood Dairy Festival. At eight, she competed in her first pageant, the Miss Talent Central States contest. She performed the song "I'm a Brass Band," (no tape of this exists, that anyone knows of). She sang, danced, and did some fancy gymnastics as well. Four states competed, Texas, Alabama, Mississippi, and Britney's home state, Louisiana. Not only did she win in the seven-to-nine-year-old category, but she swept the overall competition, with contestants three to 18 years old, as well. Victory was in the air when she received a perfect score of 120 points accumulated from the four judges. After winning another talent show (this time the Miss Talent USA) in which she sang the song, "There, I've Said It Again," she secured a spot on *Star Search*. Though some say an agent helped her book the gig, others say it was thanks to the contest. Either way, she came home a champ having won the competition. Newspaper clippings and photos show a young blond-haired Britney holding a huge mike, dressed conservatively in a black prom-like dress with velvety white material draped over her shoulders, and a black bow in her hair. It's all very sweet. This was her first national public performance, and you can bet she loved every minute of it.

Burst Bubble

Britney's first taste of disappointment came when she was eight. A friend of her mother's heard about a kids' show that was taping in Atlanta, Georgia. It was a remake of an old American favorite TV variety classic from the fifties. It was called "The Mickey Mouse Club." Knowing her friend's daughter had a love of music and a desire to perform, she suggested the two go down and audition at an open call—that meant anyone and everyone was free to try out for the show. Lynn didn't waste a second, and after a quick family discussion, she and Britney packed a few things and flew down to see if a pair of big, black ears and a large name tag were in her future. The number of kids auditioning with Britney was a little more than 600. Even though the audition was overwhelming and filled with sheer confusion, Britney made it through several cuts. Hours later she found herself competing for a spot on the show with only six other kids. She had beat out more than 90 percent of the competition. But in the final round, it was ultimately determined that because of her age, she was just too young, and she didn't book the gig. Britney was devastated. But fate has a way of working out and sometimes things do happen for the best. Though Britney was too young for her own TV series, she was too talented to overlook. A producer of the MMC, Mickey Mouse Club, knew Britney had potential. Even though he couldn't offer a job with the show at the time, he helped the budding singer's dream come true by getting her an agent in New York.

New York Anyone?

For a young girl who had never really traveled anywhere except the next town, this was an awfully big move. But Britney wasn't scared. She was thrilled. She couldn't wait to get to the Big Apple. And like Disneyland, New York has a reputation for making dreams come true and stars out of nobodies. Britney hoped that New York City luck would come to her. And so she and her mom set off to find fame and glory. "I realize I'm a little different. I need to sing. I love to travel and I've been lucky to be able to take those interests and incorporate them into my life," she says to a reporter.

Go-See

The next three summers were spent in hot, sticky Manhattan; during the rest of the year Britney was back in Kentwood with her family. Having a career meant a lot of back-and-forth traveling, but Britney didn't mind. Rather, she lived for school breaks. In New York, June, July and August were spent studying ballet, jazz, and any other kind of movement imaginable at the Off-Broadway Dance Center. She also trained at the Professional Performing Arts School. Anyone ever see the movie

Fame? In existence since 1990, PPA offers a variety of disciplines: dance, music, and drama. Kids, grades 6-12, who live in the five boroughs of New York City are accepted into the school by audition only. "We have an array of student levels. Those that are never going to get anywhere to those who are working on Broadway doing eight shows a week," says one teacher. "It's really that broad." Academics like math and history are done in the morning, and performance classes like musical theater and acting are taken in afternoon. PPA is the only school in the city that allows kids to work professionally while being in school. For Britney, this was the perfect life. She settled into her new routine with ease, enjoying the dance classes, thrilled at the prospect of auditioning for professional gigs.

When she wasn't in school she was going on "gosees," auditions she received through her agent. During her New York stay she booked some commercials: Days Inn, Mauls Barbecue Sauce, and Bell South, to name a few. But a real breakthrough came in 1991. She went on an audition for an Off Broadway show called *Ruthless*. The part Britney was to read for was for the role of Tina a so-called good girl turned evil.

Naughty Girl

Ruthless was the wacky, campy musical remake of the 1955 film *The Bad Seed*. It's the story about a little girl who appears to be nice, but is really a deadly diva in the making. Halfway through the show, she tries to kill another child because she wants the lead part in the school play. Breaking away from her good girl persona, Britney got to try her hand at adapting a character role rather removed from her personality. "At ten I was playing this really bad child who seems real sweet but she's evil," she admits to a reporter. "It was so much fun."

"The little girl is from the Midwest and sings and dances like a dream," says Donna English who played Tina's mother in the show. "She really wants the lead in the school play *Pippi in Tahiti*, so she kills off the little girl so she can have the part."

Britney wasn't cast as the lead at first. Instead, she played the part of Pippi in the showcase production. For part of her costume, Britney had to wear her hair in braids with wires sticking out: not a good look for anyone. After the workshop, she moved with the production to an Off-Broadway theater and became the understudy for the lead. (FYI: *Star Wars: The Phantom Menace* actress Natalie Portman became the understudy when Britney left the show after eight months.) "Britney was very sweet. She was wholesome, cute, unpretentious, and very normal," Donna recalls, thinking back to her *Ruthless* days. "She looked as if she was having a good time and seemed to enjoy being around the theater and learning the process. She was very pretty and had thick bangs. Some of the understudies had stage moms, but Britney's mom was very nice." The original pianist on the show felt the same way. "I remember her being a very sweet and charming girl," says Joe Thalken.

Ruthless opened in March 1991, which meant Britney would miss a semester or more of school. Being a concerned parent, Lynn arranged for Britney's school to fax homework and lesson plans to them while they were in New York. Even with her busy performance schedule, Britney kept up her studies. She also stayed in constant contact with her friends and family, briefing them on what was going on and sharing exciting stories from the East Coast.

Halfway through the show, Britney's teacher Mrs. Hughes received a postcard from the child actress that read "Dear Ms. Hughes. I miss you. I went to the July 4th parade and show and saw the fireworks. They are pretty in life." To add a creative flair, she signed her name by drawing a heart with an I in it. How cute is that?

The first number in *Ruthless* is called "Born to Entertain," and part of Britney's role was to sing her lungs out while tap dancing on a coffee table.

Talk about life imitating art. This was so appropriate; after all, "born to entertain" was the story of her life. It was like her personal motto, and a little look into the future.

The production ran through January 1992 of the following year and then closed. Britney left the production after eight months, returning home in time for Christmas and to start the New Year.

Coming of Age

Birthdays are important at any age—they mean presents, cake, candy, and everyone having to be really nice to you, and singing Happy Birthday—really loudly and off-key. But for Britney, turning 11 meant something more: It was a rite of passage. Eleven meant she was finally old enough to try out for MMC again. Hopes were high, fingers were crossed, and breath was held. Once again her mother and she boarded a plane, desperately wanting to bring back those famous ears. But this time they flew to New York for the audition, even though the show would be taping in Orlando, Florida. It seemed like one long déjà vu. Britney was as nervous as could be. But now she had credits under her belt and an impressive resume that read better than those of many New York actors struggling to break into the business. And she had had training. Once again she found herself in a large room with producers, casting agents, and important people she would have to impress to win the role over of all the other kids who wanted to wear Mickey's ears. This time luck was with her. This time, she didn't come home empty-handed. This time, she was going home to pack for yet another adventure. "It was like a dream come true," Britney shares with the *New Orleans Times Picayune*, "It was all I'd really wanted since I was eight. They called on the phone and said, 'You're going to be a Mouseketeer,' and I just started screaming and jumping up and down."

"One opportunity for Britney seems to have led rather smoothly to another," says her mom during an interview. "Really, this is the most unplanned thing you've ever seen in your life. It was as though I was mindless and things just happened." Mindless or not, the Mickey Mouse Club was an opportunity of a lifetime for Britney, one the Spears knew they couldn't pass up. Britney, her mom, and her sister who was only two at the time, packed their bags and headed off to the funnest place on earth: Disney World! Her dad and brother, who was a junior in high school at the time, held down the fort in Kentwood.

The Disney clan is something most kids can say they've been initiated into, and becoming part of it is an honor. For the second time in her short life, Britney would be leaving school, her home, and those who loved her. But she wasn't coming to Florida alone. She would be adopted into a new fun-loving family.

5

M-I-C, K-E-Y, M-O-U-S-E

The year was 1955: Dwight Eisenhower was president, Hula-Hoops were the hottest thing around and the Disney company was starting a new show, *The Mickey Mouse Club*. Back then, TV was still a rarity, and the only two colors on the screen were black and white. There was no Nintendo, no MTV, no computers with Internet capabilities and CD's were something you got at the bank. Life, in a word, was Dullsville. The Mickey Mouse Club was a much-talked-about kids' variety show. And you can imagine how much the world needed a little entertainment. The show consisted of 39 cast members and ran for four years, from 1955 to 1959.

The first Mouseketeer to win the hearts of American viewers was Annette Funicello. She was a shy, unknown 12-year-old when Walt Disney showed up during a recital at her Los Angeles dancing school. Disney fell in love with Annette and decided to cast her in the new TV series.

Thirty-eight years later, Britney was the new heartbreaker and the youngest member for *The All New Mickey Mouse Club*.

But getting on *The Mickey Mouse Club* wasn't quite as simple for Britney as it had been for Annette. She had to compete against 15,000 youngsters trying out in 13 cities throughout the United States and Canada. Her second audition was exactly three years and a day after her first. Talk about karma. She was one of seven selected to be Mouseketeers, joining the 13 cast members from the season before. It was during her MMC days that she realized what made her most happy. "We got to sing, dance, and act," Britney remarks during an interview. "That's when I realized I love to sing the best, and I love to perform. That's what I really wanted to focus on." At home she was used to being the middle child, but on MMC, Britney was the baby. "I was the youngest on the show, and I was catered to," she shares in an interview. Let's just say she had an all-around cushy job. Disney World *alone* is a lot of fun, but when you're part of the coolest, hippest show in TV land, life is more than fun; it's super cool. The show became an after-school classic and has a cult following among many old and young fans even today.

But life wasn't a total breeze. She still had to juggle rehearsals, performance, and schoolwork. The demands of a Mouseketeer are kind of high.

"We require a lot from our cast members: acting, singing, dancing, and the indefinable fourth quality of personality," says Lynne Symons, who was the director of original programming for the Disney Channel. "Britney had all four requirements." That's our star!

How It Works

Sticking with a similar formula as the original—if something's not broken, don't fix it—the show was a half-hour mixture of songs, dances, and skits. The logo, name, and basic format of the show, and the words to its theme song, stayed the same. But since it was almost four decades later, for the show to work, changes had to happen. That meant the new show had to be more hip. This time the Mouseketeers didn't wear mouse ears and uniforms. Instead they wore colorful, stylish clothes. Unfortunately the kids didn't get to pick them out themselves. They didn't even get to keep them. How rude! They did sing the old theme, "M-I-C— see you real soon—K-E-Y—Why? Because we like you—M-O-U-S-E," but they followed that with a song with a more groovy beat. "The club's got it goin' on funky style. MMC's got it goin' on funky style. We've got it goin' on with a funky style. Club scenes goin' up and the house is goin' wild." And as Britney remarks in an interview,

"It's more hip-hop now. Before, it was more little girlish."

Some of the numbers and songs Britney performed were: *Misled, I'll Take You There* (with Justin Timberlake), *Can't Help Falling in Love With You, Born To Be Wild, I Want You, I Feel For You*, and other top 20 hits pertaining to the coinciding year. She also performed in silly *Saturday Night Live*-like sketches as well. *My Big Brother Can Take Your Big Brother, The Fraidy Bunch, Kung Fu Klassics, Pig Boy, Note Passing, The Little Sisters Talk Show, Elvis Today, Parent Alarm, Interview with David Lascher, Cranko's Movie Master, and Marty & Ted's Wackee Golf,* to name a few.

This time, the cast was a multiethnic bunch as opposed to the original show. The new show also tackled some serious social issues. A special hour-long segment celebrating the 200th broadcast, for example, was devoted to positive messages about race relations. Everything about the show was a hippish-PC.

The All New Mickey Mouse Club aired in 1988 and ran for seven seasons. Britney appears in the last two. In all the years and seasons of the entire show, Britney is the only Mouseketeer from Louisiana. And since the show has not resumed, she still holds that honor.

Being among 20 young entertainers who, like herself, had been immersed in show biz from an early age, Britney felt comfortable and at ease from the very beginning. "In Orlando, all the kids are like you, they'll do all the stuff that you do," Britney divulges in an interview. "When you go to school up here (in Kentwood), none of the people are like you." Her classmates were 'teers like herself, or other child performers.

As with soap operas and regular TV series, scenes were taped non-sequentially. The skits and songs were then aired on different days. So if you shot the first song of a new episode in the morning on Monday, it might get edited into the middle of another show and air a whole month or so later. Songs and dance numbers were also assigned on a democratic basis. None of the cast had anything written for them specifically. Instead, the show's segments were written and then assigned by the director. It was a shared thing, equal and fair to all. Fifty-fifty was Mickey's deal, and it worked.

MMC was really laid-back. According to Britney, she was pampered and well taken care of. She was also on an unusual work schedule; she worked for six months and then went home for the other half of the year. On her off months she would return home happy to see everyone but antsy to get back to the glam life of TV. It seemed that this hometown girl was spreading her roots.

A normal day for an MMC-er was well structured. You received a call-time, the time you needed to be on the set, which was around 9:00

A.M. In the film biz, that's a really late time. Many TV shows tape at 7:00 A.M. or earlier, but since kids were the principal actors, (the stars), special work rules were in effect, so the show started later in the morning. At 9:00 A.M. Mouseketeers would stumble onto the set, often bleary-eyed and tired from the day before, or from late-night talks in the hotel. Then they'd be whisked off to wardrobe, get into costume, have their hair and makeup done and wait for their scene to be called. Some of the kids would rehearse during this waiting period. Others would study homework with a tutor; some just hung out. Around them, however, the stage was a blizzard of action and motion. Cameras would be set up, scenes were blocked out, and lights prepped. The director and producer would make last-minute changes in the show by cutting or adjusting some scenes and adding new ones. By 12:00-ish the cast would break for a half hour lunch. Around 12:30 P.M. things would zip into gear, mostly because they were behind from getting a late start. During the day there would be a few intermissions here and there, the kids might retire to their dressing rooms and rest but they could be called back to the stage at a moment's notice. They'd sing, dance, and study until the show broke for dinner at 5:00 P.M. They'd chow down fast and need to be back on the set to finish taping. By 6:30, the show was officially over and the director or assistant director would call "Wrap! Entire cast." The day was finished, and everyone was shuttled back to the hotel and prepared for the next day where new songs were taught and new dances were choreographed. It was pretty busy schedule, but Britney thrived on it.

Annette Funicello, Move Over

The Mickey Mouse Club may have started in the Fifties, but it's had several incarnations since. Like Freddie Kruger or another *Scream* sequel, the Mickey Mouse ears have been brought back to life three separate times, each with new casts. The next installment came in the Seventies and introduced America to new talent like snooty *Facts of Life*-r, Blair Warner, played by Lisa Welchel. Remember her? How about the name Tootie? Ring any bells? In the Eighties MMC introduced us to Britney, plus a slew of other superstars. Even though there was only a handful of kids on the show, they were all headed for fame. Most of them went on to become household names. This go-round MMC introduced us to stars like Christina Aguilera; WB's Felicity Porter, Keri Russell; JC and Justin of 'N Sync, and others.

Christina Aguilera

By the time Christina reached her thirteenth birthday, she had already been an MMC-er and featured vocalist for two seasons. Like Britney, Christina also appeared on *Star Search*, but when she was eight, Britney was ten. She recently returned to her old roots when she recorded for Disney the song "Reflection," which was in the summer 1998 animated feature, *Mulan*. To get the job, Christina made a demo using a simple tape recorder. Her makeshift audition tape was all Chris Montan needed to hear. The search was over. Forty-eight hours and 3,000 miles later, Christina was in a Los Angeles recording studio singing out her interpretation of "Reflection." For the past several months she's been preparing for the release of her new album, released in March. Recently, she performed at the Golden Stag Festival in Romania along with Diana Ross and Sheryl Crow. Her days with MMC are vividly burned in her memory. "Becoming a Mouseketeer was the happiest moment in my life," says Christina, in an MMC interview. They were good memories, it seems, for all the kids.

Keri Russell

Another successful star to have come out of the MMC group was WB's Felicity, Keri Russell. "She was older and basically stuck with the older kids," Britney remarks in *Girl's Life*. "She's so sweet. She's such a beautiful person." The two may not have been as close as she and Christina were, but Keri certainly made her own mark, being the first one to make a name in films and TV. Keri's experience was much like Annette's: Two talent scouts took a sneak look at the native Californian. In 1990 they found her doing some fancy dance moves in an acting studio where she was taking some classes. She was 14 at the time. After the show ended, Keri went on to star in several movies, her first being Disney's *Honey I Blew Up The Kid*. She guest-starred and became a regular on TV series such as MMC's spin-off series, *Emerald Cove*, *Boy Meets World*, *Clerks*, and *Married . . . With Children*. She had a fleeting part on a short lived sitcom called *Daddy's Girl* with Dudley Moore, which wasn't very funny, and a larger part on Aaron Spelling's *Malibu Shores*. Her most famous commercial was for Noxema— clean face, great skin, that's Keri. But it wasn't this major slew of work that got her recognized, it was a TV show called *Felicity* that put Keri in college, and on the map. She still loves music and dancing and whenever her work schedule permits, she attends rock concerts. Today, Keri lives in Los Angeles with her cat, Nala.

Ryan Gosling

Ryan was 12 years old when MMC took him aboard. At first Ryan's mother was hesitant to let him get involved in professional show business. "She didn't want it to have any bad effects on me," Ryan explains to *Bop*. Eventually she agreed to let him follow his heart. Ryan later went on to work in two films, *Nothing's Too Good for a Cowboy* and *Frankenstein and Me*. That was just the beginning. It seemed that Ryan had the Midas touch. Everything he auditioned for, he booked. First he landed a recurring role on the television series *Adventures of Shirley Holmes* and went on to appear in numerous television series, including *Road to Avonlea, Goosebumps, Are You Afraid of the Dark?* and *Flash Forward*. His career kicked into overdrive when, in 1997, he won the role of Sean Hanlon on USA's *Breaker High*. Earlier this year Ryan nabbed the role of a lifetime in his current gig as Hercules in the Fox Kids Network's *Young Hercules*. Now 17-year-old Ryan spends a great deal of time across the globe in New Zealand because that's where *Young Hercules* is filmed, but he goes back home to Canada on his hiatus to visit friends and family.

*　　*　　*

Aside from the discipline and training MMC gave Britney, the show also introduced her to two very special, awesomely cute, and totally irresistible guys who would later play a major part in her life. Can you guess who these lucky fellas were? Yup. You're right. Score—a direct hit.

Little Justin Randall Timberlake and JC Chasez

"Justin and I were picked together to be on the show," Britney tells *MTV News*. "But JC had already been on the show for almost two years before I was chosen."

Originally from Memphis, Justin met Britney on the first day of auditions. And thanks to MMC, Justin was the first boy Britney ever kissed. "Pretty is cool but it's not really about looks for me, it's more about personality," Justin openly says in an interview about his ideal gal. "I like a girl with a good sense of humor, who's humble and sensitive." Like Britney, he was one of the youngest kids on MMC.

JC was from Bowie, Maryland, and was superhyper. Even though he had lots of spunk, he also had a big heart. When he was on the show, his philosophy was "Treat people the way you want to be treated." What impressed him most about being on MMC were the wonderful friends he made. "It's incredible to meet performers who are just the nicest people in the world and are so down to earth," says JC in an old interview back from his MMC days. It seems like Britney was in good company. But we'll get back to these boys later.

When the cast wasn't taping the show or doing homework, Britney and the rest of the talented troupe hung out by the pool, had meals together, and stayed at the same apartment complex. Between free time, work, and performances, intense friendships were formed.

Even though Britney hasn't seen some of her fellow 'teers in a while, she keeps tabs on her fellow mouse alumni. She had all the goop on Ryan, and her old pal Christina. In fact, she and Christina were very close as kids; they were best friends. Back in an old MMC interview, they were asked what they liked best about each other: Christina answers, "She can always make me smile and feel good about myself." Britney came back with kudos about Chris. "She's very honest, down to earth, and a good friend." Though the girls don't get to see much of each other now that both have full-time music careers, they have still kept their friendship alive. They recently saw each other over the holiday break. "I had dinner with Britney in New York. That was cool," Christina says. "I hadn't seen her since MMC. It was a great feeling that our friendship is as strong as ever." Britney, of course, feels the same way.

Dear Britney

Part of a Mouseketeer's job was to answer fan mail. Each week gigantic bags would be delivered to the Disney lot. Even at 12,. Britney was level-headed, quick, and great at giving advice. Here are some letters from *The Mickey Mouse Club* that Britney answered and the helpful tips she gave to stressed out teens.

"I like this guy and I think he likes me. I'm tempted to ask him out on a date but I'm too shy. The other problem is my friends don't think he's cute, even though I do. I know I shouldn't care what they think, but I'm afraid they'll make fun of him. One of my friends told me he has a girlfriend, but I don't know if that's true."

Britney's fabulous answer? "First, I think you should find out if he has a girlfriend. Then find out if he likes you. If he asks you to go out with him and you really like him, say yes. It doesn't matter what your friends say, it's what you say. Do what you think is right."

Sounds like good advice. Another stuck fan wrote *"I like a guy in my class named Ryan. He seems to like me, but I'm not sure. I used to go out with a guy named Chris, who is now my best friend. Chris says he wants to go out with me again, but I really like Ryan. I don't want to hurt Chris. What should I do?''*

"Find out if Ryan likes you. Then figure out which boy you like best. Try to stay friends with the boy you like less. If he doesn't want to stay friends with you, then you made a good choice in picking the boy you like." That's our levelheaded pop queen.

The Party's Over

Nothing lasts forever, and MMC was no different. After Britney had worked on the show for two years, it got canceled. Some say the producers of MMC were expecting to make a splash with the new sixth season cast members, but ratings didn't quite take off as they had hoped. Others say many of the 'teers were graduating or about to graduate from high school. Many cast members wanted to try their hand at films and other TV projects. Even though the kids were under contract for an additional two seasons, they were released and production ended on October 22, 1994.

Disappointed but ready for a change, Britney returned home to her family and friends. And a normal life resumed. Well, as normal as life for a former Mouseketeer can be. Because she had been so busy, her schedule filled with a multitude of activities, rehearsals, and performances, it was no wonder she was bored stupid when she got home. During these two years the one thing that hadn't changed was her dream. "It was fun for a while, but I started getting itchy to get out again and see the world," she shares with an interviewer. "I've always wanted to be a singer. It's all I've wanted to do since I was five," The taste for stardom and a love for music was still inside her, and it had gotten stronger.

Back at the Ranch

At 14, Britney was back in Louisiana and had completed one year of high school. Though she had just come from TV land, people didn't treat her much differently back at home. She and her friends resumed as if nothing had ever happened. "Coming from such a small town, everyone knew me before," she tells *Girl's Life*. Sometimes recognition did happen. "A fan would come up to me and say they had seen me on TV," she adds. Other than that, life was calm and status quo.

While at home, Britney filled her social calendar with the regular stuff. She went on dates with guys, but many were just friends, she hung out at the mall and shopped till she dropped, still a favorite pastime of Britney's today. She goofed around, acted silly, saw movies, read books, did homework, and had family dinners with her folks and siblings—but life was, well, humdrum and kind of boring for the 'teer who was used to a totally filled schedule. Her restlessness grew more and more each day. "I was antsy and needed adventure and to perform," she tells an interviewer. She missed her MMC friends, the singing, dancing, rehearsals, and intense atmosphere. "That's when my dad called Larry Rudolph," she informs *Entertainment Weekly*. Larry was a high-powered New York entertainment lawyer who had some mighty big connections. He told her dad that pop music was coming back and suggested that Britney send him a tape of her singing. Great idea! Only one problem, Britney didn't have a demo tape. Even with all the video tapes of her in MMC, she didn't have anything with just her singing the kind of songs she wanted to sing. Mom came to the rescue and with a little help and a lot of blank audiotapes, they made a makeshift demo on the family recorder. That was the best they could do, and they hoped Larry would take into account that they didn't have many resources in their area available to them. Her mom sent the demo to Larry, and they crossed their fingers. They didn't have to wait long. When Larry heard the tape, he was ecstatic. And without having to think too hard, he signed up as her manager. Suddenly another person had joined the Spears crew, a captain.

Hit the Road, Jack

And so at 15, bags were packed once more, good-byes said, and tears shed. Britney was becoming an excellent packer. Her mom was, too. In fact the whole thing had begun to feel routine and normal. She came back to New York once more to find her shining star and her place in the world. This time she'd find more than anyone could ever have expected.

6

The Making of a Star

An Unconventional Lifestyle

By now, Britney had traded in her Mickey Mouse ears and pompoms for the next step; a life-long career in music. Once back in the big city she auditioned for all sorts of gigs including an all-girl vocal band (the Spice Girls they weren't). She got the job, but lasted only one day with the group. "They couldn't get their dance numbers together," she explains to *Teen Celebrity*. "They didn't even have a name."

For a batch of cookie dough to taste just right it needs several major ingredients: sugar, eggs, milk, and most important, chocolate chips. Becoming a star takes the same—no chocolate necessary, but candy always helps. For someone to make it big she needs talent, ambition, drive, people in her corner, and a major plan. Britney had all of that. The big secret component? A small record company called Jive.

At the same time Britney's so-called singing group was coming together, Larry, her manager, had sent her demo to Jeff Sincer, VP of A&R for Jive Records. "She sang over an instrumental that wasn't in her key," confides Jeff to *Billboard magazine*. "But I heard something special. Her vocal ability and commercial appeal caught me right away." Jive invited her to audition in a conference room filled with bigwigs and major executives. As with a college interview where the dean and top five teachers are seated at a table staring at you, looking over your application, Britney had to sparkle, shine, and sound like a million bucks. The pressure was on. "I was really nervous," she admits to one reporter. "It's easy to sing in front of a thousand people because you can't really see their faces. But then you go into a room, and there are ten people staring at you . . ." That could make anyone crazed.

Up to the challenge, Britney prepared and thought positively. She chose to audition with a song by her mentor, Whitney Houston, "I Have Nothing." Not an easy tune to sing, and a challenge for any seasoned singer. For an encore, she performed one of Mariah Carey's hits. Of course, she blew them away. Everyone loved her. Jive signed her on the spot. Even though she walked in with a homemade tape, she walked out with a contract—an opportunity of a lifetime.

Without missing a beat, Jeff signed her to a

development deal. "It's very rare that we sign someone without a proper demo," he admits to *Hit Sensations*, "but once we heard her sing in our office we offered her a deal right on the spot. I was so impressed that she made it happen on her own. It wasn't just handed to her."

"Britney is a fascinating person to be around," says one record label insider in a recent article. "On one hand she's very much still a refreshing kid who's got a great outlook on life. On the other hand she is a very dedicated professional who is willing to do whatever needs to be done to make sure her career will go in the direction she wants. I feel confident that in 10, 20, even 30 years from now she'll still be making great music. That's the kind of talent she is."

Everything was happening so fast Britney's head was spinning. One minute she was just a Midwestern girl, going to school, hanging with friends, attending church functions. The next, she was signing contracts and set to record an album. She could hardly believe her luck. Her family and friends continued to cheer her on and lend their support even though they were so far away. She was most definitely on her way.

Sign On The Dotted Line.

For the next year, all of Britney's efforts would go into making her CD. Her first stop was Sweden and for a girl who loves to travel she couldn't have wished for a better place. She had never been to Europe, or any other foreign country, for that matter. Mainly her traveling had included Florida, Georgia, and New York. Britney was probably packed weeks in advance.

Work went into overdrive, and Britney was wisked off to Sweden's Cherion Studios, where 'N Sync, Robyn, Ace of Base, and the Backstreet Boys had all laid their voices on the tape and created their hip-hop, supersonic, contagious sound.

It was in Sweden where she met Max Martin, the man who wrote "... Baby One More Time." Things went really well in Europe. The deal was to record three songs for the album within the allotted ten-day period, but on a roll, they ended up cutting six numbers instead. For a girl who loves to travel and sightsee, Britney didn't get a chance to see anything, let alone have a photo op in the glamorous country. Even though she spent close to two weeks in Sweden, she worked the whole time. If you listen really carefully, you can probably guess which songs were recorded there. Britney says she can. The difference being some have a little European snap to them. Max, the guy responsible for giving the Backstreet Boys their signature sound, wrote and co-produced Britney's album. "He's incredible," says Britney of her Max. "They went to the next level with me. He's awesome." And he thinks the same of her. "She's got an excellent voice. It's what I heard in the BSB. She's got a good sense of catching the melody, performing it, and taking it to another level. Because as a songwriter that's what you're looking for," Max says in an interview. Max has also produced other super stars such as: Ace of Base, Robyn, Bop Boys, and E-Type. He's worked as a mixer, engineer, arranger, and even lent his vibrato to several of the records he's supervised. He's also been nominated for several Grammys. But there's more. Give the guy a pen and watch out. A hit song is just a piece of paper away. Max is the brainchild behind, "As Long As You Love Me," "Everybody," "That's The Way I Like It," "10,000 Promises," "Quit Playing Games With My Heart," and several of Britney's hip-hop songs.

Next enter Eric Foster White, the song man and producer extraordinaire, who had produced and written material for big hitters like Hi-Five, Boyzone, and one of Britney's heroes, Witney Houston. He was immediately taken with the budding star. "It came together rather quickly, an unusual experience for a solo pop album," shares Eric with *Billboard*. "It was a case of good chemistry among a group of very talented people. The writers and producers immediately saw what we at the label did."

Having a fondness for instruments, Eric plays nearly everything one can imagine: keyboard, drums, bass, even the trombone. As an arranger and producer, he's recorded and written for Lee Levin, Josh Grau, Hi-Five, Countess Vaughn, and Roz Davis. Even though some of those names and groups might still be unfamiliar, at this moment, Eric is considered hot, hot, hot.

It was in a New Jersey studio where the other five songs were recorded. In fact, the studio soon became Britney's calling card. If you needed to know where she was you could check the recording box. "It's my second home," she confides in a recent article.

Love at First Sound

Britney had been in the studio for days, listening to lots of material and recording stuff that she liked a lot, but hadn't fallen too head-over-heels for. Where was the hit? Where was the Number 1? What was going to put her on the charts? The answer came to her in Sweden while she was working with Max. He played Britney a demo tape for a song called "... Baby One More Time." And history was made. Bells rang, sirens roared, and lights flashed. They had finally found a winner. "I knew from the start," Britney excitedly recalls to *Billboard*, "that it was one of those songs you want to hear again and again. It just felt really right." She went into the studio and made the song her own "trying to give it a little more attitude than the demo." She was beyond excited. She knew deep inside that she had a hit. Max, her producers and the folks at Jive all felt the synergy starting.

Originally, Max and Britney were scheduled to cut only two songs together. But the two felt such chemistry, they ended up recording five of the cuts. Now that's a steamy collaboration. Put that with the three she did in New Jersey, and you've got the 11 songs that appear on her self-titled CD.

In an industry where tempers fly, egos bruise easily, and people walk off projects in the blink of an eye, Britney was considered a sweetie-pie. It was evident that everyone thus far had enjoyed working with her. It was just like school—everyone wanted to be her friend. But this time, Britney didn't cry and she got to play with everyone. With Max and Eric behind her 100 percent, Britney couldn't lose. Things were really coming together.

To Market, To Market, To Create a Big Star

Jack Spear, a senior V.P. of pop promotions and jive records, has worked with tons of artists over the years, but never with one as special and talented as Britney. He even went so far as to compare the prodigy to a young Madonna, stating that Jive's goal was to create a pop-rhythm crossover singer. And that's just what they were going to do. It was all part of their big plan.

Jive wasted no time introducing Britney to the world and the world to Britney. A six-month marketing plan designed to transform a pretty girl into a sweeping sweet teen sensation went into action. "We put [a hotline] number on a post card and circulated them to the fan clubs of several major pop artists," explains Kim Kaiman, director of marketing at Jive Records. The label also set up a Website complete with pictures, videotaped interview footage, and music clips. The response was overwhelming. Kids took to Britney instantly. And who could blame them?

Three months before the single was released, Britney treaded on very familiar ground. She took to the malls of Middle America. As a girl who loves shopping almost more than singing she was in heaven. This time she got to do both. First she sang, then she shopped. It was the best combination the pop sensation could have asked for.

For her mall review, she and two dancers performed four carefully choreographed songs and handed out goodie bags. Kids stood in line, anxious to receive a sample cassette containing the songs they'd just heard. Jive knew they had a hit. After all Britney was a gifted singer who could also dance like no one they had ever seen. Jive didn't need to consult the Psychic Friends' Network. Their predictions were right on target. As in love at first sight, everyone liked what they saw.

Hip magazines like *Teen*, *Seventeen*, *Teen People*, and *YM*, and companies like Benetton and L'Oréal all took part in making Britney a celebrity. Along with Jive, they co-sponsored Britney to perform cuts of her album at 25 malls. The shows drew hundreds of kids who all fell totally ga-ga for the young ingenue. "It was crazy," Britney tells *People*. "No one knew who I was, but I could tell they really enjoyed the music." Plus she came home with her own goodie bags from her favorite shops. Not bad for a few days' work.

Picking Up Speed

Finally the day was here. According to Jive Records, the single was released on November 3. Things were going great on the mall scene, people were calling in to the music hotline to hear her songs, and word about the young artist was spreading. There had been so much planning, so much excitement and talk about the song people could hardly contain themselves around the Jive office. You could just feel as if something thrilling and large was going to happen.

". . . Baby One More Time" hit the streets on November 3, and opened on the charts on November 23, at number 17. But it didn't take long for it to hit number 1. In fact, it took only ten weeks. Everyone who heard the song loved it instantly. It was as if a huge musical spell was cast on the world.

Jive quickly sent the star out on a 30-city radio tour, showcasing her wherever it could. Mark Adams, program director at KZQZ (95.7) radio in San Francisco, recalls the star being totally pleasant and charming. She talked a blue streak and had defiant thoughts about what direction she wanted to take her career. Mark found the song so strong that even if she were rude—not our Britney—he would have played the song anyway. Hey, a hit's a hit. Sometimes you just can't stop greatness. Some people would mind being shuffled off to obscure places and small radio stations, but not Britney. She had a blast meeting people, visiting places she had never been, and was treated to gourmet food fit for royalty. "I probably gained five pounds," she jokes in an interview.

Witch Soundtrack

During all this excitement her song "Soda Pop" was added to the *Sabrina the Teenage Witch* soundtrack. *Witch* has sold over 500,000 copies. Britney joined other famous and talented artists with numbers such as The Backstreet Boys' "Hey, Mr. DJ (Keep Playin' This Song)," Robyn's "Show Me Love," 'N Sync's "Giddy Up," Five's "Slam Dunk (Da Funk)," The Cardigans' "Blah, Blah, Blah" and the Spice Girls' "Walk of Life." Even Melissa Joan Hart, the 25-year-old teenage witch star, made a vocal appearance adding "*One Way or Another*" to the album.

Sabrina the Teenage Witch airs on ABC on Friday nights at 9:00 P.M. Eastern time. Based loosely on the popular Archie comics heroine, Sabrina, the TV show's Sabrina is a modern-day sorcerer's apprentice who lives with her two eccentric aunts. Between the three, it's sheer chaos. They are always getting into trouble. When Sabrina finds out on her sixteenth birthday that she's a witch, all hell breaks lose. To make things even more complicated, Sabrina must keep her special talents a secret from her friends and everyone at school. Like *Buffy The Vampire Slayer*, she has friends and enemies: her quirky and free-spirited best friend, Jenny; her friend and potential love interest, Harvey; and Sabrina's nemesis, Libby. Her two aunts and a mischievous warlock, who's doing time as a black cat, do their best to help her along the way and stop her from getting in trouble. During each episode Sabrina finds out that wiggling your nose won't always save the day.

Born in Sayville, New York, Melissa, who at one time was best known for her comedy series *Clarissa Explains It All*, has lobbied to win guest spots on the show for some of her favorite performers to make cameo appearances. They include Coolie and the Violent Femmes. Since Britney and her CD have done so phenomenally well, maybe she'll make the witch list, too. She'd be a wonderful singing sorceress, don't you think? Maybe if we all make a wish on a rising star, it will come true.

7

In Record Time

"This is what I want," Britney tells the *Toronto Sun* of her zooming music career. " 'Cause when I was in the Mickey Mouse Club, it was so different than this. You'd wake up and you'd have your little schedule and then you'd come home. We had it made and we didn't even know it. It was like nothing at all. Even though this is harder, I'm enjoying it more because I'm growing as a person and I'm finding out things about myself that I never knew before."

LeAnne Rimes was only 13 when she conquered the country charts, Brandy was 15 when she crashed onto the R&B scene. But Britney has done the deed twice. Many girls never get this far, but then again, many girls aren't Britney. Remember the catchy young voices of Samantha Fox and Tiffany? Sure. But as they became the subjects of VH-1 and MTV's where-are-they-now? shows, Britney took center stage once more breaking all kinds of records and blowing her predecessors out of the water and off the hit parade charts.

Why is the world totally ready to accept a new artist? Maybe Britney has the answer. "There was a while when there was no pop music on the radio," she explains to a reporter. "All you heard was rock and adult contemporary. I don't know. I just think people like the sound of pop music more than ever."

While the single was zooming up the charts to Number 1, Britney and Jive were getting ready to release her long-awaited album. Receiving much publicity and notoriety for the *Sabrina* soundtrack and from the mall appearances and radio spots, this kid was a star before the album was delivered. Excitement and anticipation was felt by all. The minute the album was released it went straight to Number 1, breaking all kinds of records.

Fast Track

"My favorite song is probably ' . . . Baby One More Time,' because it's a fun song, but it has attitude and an edge to it which makes it different." Her other fave? " 'From the Bottom of My Broken Heart.' It's a special song because it's one of the first songs I did when I got signed to Jive. And usually, the first song you do when you get signed to a record label, they end up forgetting about," she tells a reporter.

As if the music alone isn't enough, each CD comes with a fold-out poster of Britney, sitting backwards on a chair in a baby-T and jeans, plus four smaller shots, each with her looking totally cute and sexy. In case you've missed an on-air TV or radio appearance—yeah right—and don't know what her voice sounds like when she's not singing, it can be heard at the end of the last cut. In a perky, chipper voice she shares with her listener a sneak preview of the newest album from her famous labelmates, the Backstreet Boys. Hearing her genuinely excited inflection, you can't help wanting to rush right out and buy the album, as if doing so would be performing a personal favor for Britney. There are also lyrics to four songs, ". . . Baby One More Time," "Sometimes," "Born To Make You Happy," and "From The Bottom Of My Broken Heart," as if you needed to look, which are included inside the cover. And don't forget the enclosed catalog of Britney merchandise, all of which is fashionable and cute. It won't be long before teens don her T-shirt and sport her fishing hat. Need something to keep your keys together? Order her keychain. Want to look cool in the hot sun? Put on her white-ribbed-in-blue halter top. Or slip into her baby-T—of course it's baby blue—Britney's fave color—or her red spaghetti-strap tank. For those who like a long-sleeve shirt, fear not—one comes in navy blue. It's a veritable Britney wardrobe.

Fan club info, as well as e-mail addresses for Britney and Eric, can all be found inside the CD, too.

Once you hear her songs, you can't help but fall in love. Before you know it you're singing along with her sultry, baby-doll voice, a sweet combination of two of her favorite artists, Whitney Houston and Mariah Carey. And Britney sounds like the perfect blend of both, with a little of her own style and sound added for a unique mix. The album is a mastery of songs. Soulful at times, a little country at others with a Jamaican ditty here and there—all help to add shape and color. Hip-hop tunes and dance numbers give it attitude, the ballads make it a classic. Lastly the famous Sonny and Cher calypso remix gives it eclectic funk. It's a no-brainer why this CD is such a hit.

What's In a Song

Her signature song, ". . . Baby One More Time," is "about a girl that's dating this guy and they break up, which she regrets, and she needs a sign that they can get back together," she tells Zoo Disney. "Soda Pop," a reggae-oriented song by Eric Foster, is like "a party song," she discloses to a reporter. "It's that song you get ready to before you go out at night." Mike Basie added the reggae thing and made it, well, pop. "And The

Beat Goes On'' was her least favorite song at the time the album was released. The Sonny and Cher hit, ''And the Beat Goes On,'' was a tune Britney was unfamiliar with. It wasn't until she was at a photo shoot where her CD was playing that she was sold on it. ''Everyone was older than me and went 'I love that,' '' she states. That was all she needed. ''You Drive Me Crazy,'' ''Sometimes,'' ''Born To Make You Happy,'' ''I Will Be There''—a little ''Mmmmbop''-ish, ''I Will Still Love You,'' ''Thinkin' About You,'' and ''E-mail My Heart'' complete the 11 songs recorded for her first album. The final song Britney talks openly about is ''From The Bottom Of My Heart,'' a soft ballad. ''This song is one of those songs that just stays with you. It's just a really nice song about your first love. Every girl can relate to that,'' says Britney to *MTV News*. But that is the basis for all of Britney's songs. That's actually her goal. Singing and writing songs people can connect to.

A last minute contender, that didn't make the cut was ''Autumn Good-bye,'' which is not listed on her album. As Britney puts it, it's ''kind of like an end of the summer romance when you meet somebody when school's out or you are on vacation and you have to say good-bye to that romance when school starts again in autumn,'' Britney informs Zoo Disney. It would be no surprise to find it on her second CD or perhaps on the B-side of her next single.

A Song of Her Own

Speaking of a next release . . . "Sometimes," the third song on her CD has the attitude and personal style of Britney. That's mostly because she supposedly wrote the words to it. "Yeah, actually I wrote the B-side for the second single, which is going to be 'Sometimes.' The B-side is called 'I'm So Curious.' I wrote the lyrics and the melody for that," she shares with a reporter. She started writing a lot when she was recording her album. The video for "Sometimes" will be directed by Nigel Dick, the guy who shot ". . . Baby One More Time." The new clip will show Britney on the porch of a beachfront home in Malibu watching a group of kids having fun, which will prompt flashbacks about her former boyfriend. Now *that's* hot.

Hitting Rock Top

"I was in West Palm Beach and I was sleeping," Britney recalls during an interview. "My lawyer called me along with the president of Jive and they said, 'Are you sitting down? Are you ready for this?' I was half asleep and when they told me I thought they were talking about the single.'' In reality, they were telling her that the album had debuted at Number 1. "I totally flipped out. It was really awesome."

Britney Spears the CD exploded onto the charts. "Jive recording artist Britney Spears has taken the music world by storm and debuts simultaneously on *Billboard*'s Top 200 Albums and on the Hot 100 Singles charts at the Number 1 position" reads *Entertainment Wire*. Selling over 115,000 copies in its first week of release, ". . . Baby One More Time" is one of the few songs to have had such an intense and immediate response from everyone!

Britney still gets captured by surprise, forgetting that it's actually her own cool, sweet voice coming out of the speakers, and just gets caught up in the contagious beat and rhythm of the song. "Even when I hear it sometimes, I forget that's me singing, and I want to hear the song again," she states in an article. The album and planning took about a year to complete. She was only 15 when she signed with Jive, and 16 by the time her single was released, which to the antsy artist must have felt like forever. But everyone agrees, planning takes time and good things come to those who wait. History truly was made when Britney's album went to the top. She is the youngest debut artist to date to have a Number 1 single and a Number 1 album at the same time.

8

Viva la Video

Madonna may have had her bustier, Mick Jagger had those big lips, Kiss had their wacky makeup, and Michael Jackson had his moonwalk. But Britney's got the flattest abs and the most famous stomach around. She's also the only one who can make a school uniform look cool, hot, sexy, sweet, and hip all at the same time. The video for ". . . Baby One More Time," was an instant success and clicked with everyone who saw it. Requested like crazy, it's quickly gone into heavy rotation on MTV and VH-1. But some say the video's not as American-pie and innocent as one might have expected from the perfect all-American girl. Many feel the video is rather provocative: Britney dances around in a girls' private-school uniform with a short skirt, thigh-high black stockings and a white shirt tied up to expose a midriff and black bra underneath.

You can't please everyone, and Britney isn't

trying to. As long as her fans enjoy the video, her job is done. And it's been done well.

Britney is quick to shoo away any unrealistic concerns an overprotective viewer might have. "I mean, it would be different if I was walking around naked," she says, in her defense, to the *Toronto Sun*. "But that's how kids are today. I mean, where I'm from, I don't think anything of it if someone has a sports bra on and is dancing. I don't think it's like Madonna, and I'm all over someone. I think it's fun, with me wearing a little midriff top and skirt or whatever. It'd be different if my skirt was up to my ass." Did she just say "ass?" Regardless of what a few critics think, the video really helped the single to stay on the hit chart. "It helped tremendously because it's something everyone can relate to," defends Britney to a reporter. "There's a storyline with me wanting the guy back. I want something all the kids my age can relate to." Being bored in school, wanting desperately to be anywhere but there, is definitely something everyone can understand and connect with. All everyone really wants to do is run around outside in the sun, hang out, and chat with friends. That was Britney's vision, make a fun video with a lot of dancing in it. And she did just that.

". . . Baby One More Time" was directed by Nigel Dick, who also supervised radically successful musical videos for the Backstreet Boys,

Paul McCartney, Guns N' Roses, and Savage Garden. He had directed well over 200 music videos including: Matchbox 20's "Push," Oasis' "Wonderwall," Third Eye Blind's "How's It Going to Be," and "As Long As You Love Me," which helped the BSB capture more than just fame and glory. The video won the 1997 MTV Europe Select Award for Fan-Voted Favorite Video.

During Nigel's video success, he made an attempt at breaking into the film directing arena as well. By the mid-Nineties he had three movies under his belt, none of which had broken any box-office records or won any awards. *Dead Connection* was filmed in 1994, *P.I. Private Investigations* in 1997, and *Deadly Intent*, a thriller about the bad karma that follows a stolen gem from the South American jungle into the great U.S. of A. was shot in 1988. Good thing he moved to TV. He may not have had a nose for films, but he's got a great eye and wonderful ear for music videos. It was in the late 1980s that he made his mark.

Randy Conner was the choreographer who created and developed the fancy dance steps and cool movements Britney and her backup singers perform. High school never looked like this.

Two weeks of rehearsals were scheduled for the dancers, but the video itself was shot in three days in L.A. at a school where some pretty slick kids went. Remember the movie *Grease*? Rydell High, which is actually a real school called Venice High School in California, was the perfect location of the shoot. But this time there were no poodle skirts, no bobby socks or guys with greased-back hair and leather jackets. When you think about it, however, Britney is a kind of Sandra Dee, wouldn't you agree? In fact, she'd be perfect in that role, if they ever shot a remake.

Even a family member and friend got in on the act. Britney's cousin Chad, a clothing model for Abercrombie & Fitch, can be seen in a prime role, Britney's love interest. Look for him in the bleachers of the gym. Obviously, the two aren't romantically involved in real life, duh. It does pay to have the right connections—and he's a cute boy to boot.

Just when it seemed things couldn't get any better, they did. News came of a tour with five boys. Britney was beside herself with joy.

9

In Sync with 'N Sync

November 18 at the Tupperware Center in Orlando, Florida, was a magical night filled with frenzy, anticipation, and hopes of stardom as Britney embarked on a tour that would change her life, and her world, forever. Picture this: 6,000 screaming fans, five totally cute fellas and two very special opening acts. You do the math and end up with one hot and dynamic show. Giving a concert, especially when it's your fist time, can be exhilarating and overwhelming. You try getting all those crazed fans to relax and get back in their seats. This is not any easy task. But as the dust settled, and the audience quieted down, a beautiful girl took center stage filled with excitement, jitters—and poise. Cue lights, welcome Spears. Twenty minutes of material plus her own dancers, Jeri and TJ, who Britney claims are the funniest guys in the world, were all a hit from the first note. (Tania and Charissa joined the dancing trio later on.) High-powered choreography impressed the crowd as Britney performed a handful of cuts from her not-yet-released album. Before the set was over, she had everyone on their feet and dancing. Of course, she closed with "... Baby One More Time," her signature song, and received a standing ovation. Preteen spirit was everywhere, and a major celeb was born.

Every girl's dream is to tour, and what an amazing thrill and experience to tour with five cuties like the members of 'N Sync. But not all five were strangers to Britney. Remember those Mouseketeer days? Well, Britney wasn't the only one with a pair of big ears. Both Justin and JC had also been part of the Disney club, and reuniting with them was amazing. Joey (Joseph Anthony Fatone), Chris (Christopher Alan Kirkpatrick), and Lance (James Lance Bass) accepted her into the group with open arms, happy to have a girl join. Together with B*witched, the tour couldn't fail. They were the hottest show around, and the timing of Britney's opening for them couldn't have been any better. But opening for the hunks was just a stepping stone. Britney hopes to have her own tour one day, and who can blame her? "It's a big dream," she continues, "but right now, I think opening for the boys was really good." Her only concern was envy. "What I was worried about was the girls having that jealousy with me opening up for them and them loving the guys and being like 'Who is this girl? Get her off the stage, I wanna see 'N Sync,' " she tells another reporter. She was slightly anxious about opening for them in the beginning—after all, the fellas were seasoned performers, while Britney was only 16 at the time. Yet those fears were not first on her list of concerns. "I was nervous about how the crowd was going to respond because I'm just the opening act, and they're there to see 'N Sync," says Britney to Entertainment Asylum. But Britney has so much going for her, she's able to win over any crowd. "I have guy dancers and believe me, that helps." Britney's fears and concerns were nothing to bust a move for. The crowds love her, 'N Sync loves her—heck, the whole world is gaga over her. "It hasn't always been easy opening for these guys, since there are all these girls in the audience," Britney admits to *Billboard.* "It's been an incredible, intense time."

Working long hours, dancing up a storm, and learning last-minute changes is not as easy as it looks. Thanks to her MMC days and all those years of ballet training—Britney has taken all sorts of dance training, gymnastics, movement classes—she was more than able to remember her new steps. Her first time opening for 'N Sync was totally crazy. "It was kind of weird because it was my first time on stage," Britney admits during an online interview. "I was scared I was gonna forget something." But she didn't need to psych herself out, she did awesomely. "It's good to perform and everything and see the audience really know your music and get into your songs," she tells another interviewer. But that's just the tip of the appreciation charts. "The crowd's reaction is the best feeling when you're up there. Even songs that aren't out yet and they're still screaming, that's the best feeling in the world because they know your music. And they're screaming your name." From the looks and sound of it all and the tons of letters, e-mails, and fan mail she's been receiving, people will be screaming her name loud and clear for many, many years to come.

Another benefit of doing the show was working with her old pals, Justin and JC. After a long hiatus, she was pleasantly surprised by some of the changes that had transpired over the past several years. "JC has matured a lot," she explains in a recent interview. "He's quieter now. He was totally rambunctious."

Contrary to belief, life on the road is not all fun and songs. "The first week of the tour was kind of crazy because they completely crammed my schedule, and I wasn't used to the bus and everything." No homesickness went around, though, because Britney went home every six weeks to see her family. And when she's touring or on the road, she phones in everyday to speak to Mom, Dad, and friends.

As for hanging with the boys? "We actually

don't get to hang out much," she tells Entertainment Asylum. "Right now I'm busy all during the day and before the show." Still, Britney joins the quintet for many meals. "They're really nice and they're just the coolest." The guys like her, too. For her seventeenth birthday, after one of the shows in Kalamazoo, Michigan, they threw her a little party complete with flowers and balloons. They also surprised Britney by singing "Happy Birthday," a capella, I'm sure. But other than a special occasion or event, nothing terribly exciting happened backstage. When her 20-minute stage show was over, Britney would head back to the bus or her hotel and try to soak up a little R&R. "I never wait for them, because we've got to get ready for the next city." Also, 'N Sync had so many fans waiting to talk to them, Britney felt a little claustrophobic.

To pass the time on the tour bus, Britney and the boys played fun games like Truth or Dare. "We played this one game called Questions," she shares with *Girl's Life*. Each player writes down a question on a piece of paper and places in a hat. The hat is passed around the circle, and each person has to pick a slip of paper and answer the question openly and honestly, no matter what. The most personal question Britney had to answer was "How many boys have you kissed?" Blushing, she replied, "Five or six."

A brainchild, Britney juggles a career and

school work without feeling like she's missing the teenage experience. "I take a home-study program," she informs one reporter. No tutor travels with her; she does it on her own, and she just finished the tenth grade. "Sometimes it's hard to focus on school work," Britney admits. "Sometimes I'll be like, 'Oh man, I don't want to do this,' but I do it anyway." But Britney doesn't miss school one iota. "Before I did this, I'd get up in the morning, go to school, hang with my friends, and go to church. I know I had to give up stuff to do this," she confides to an interviewer. "When I was home for two years, every weekend we'd go out and do the same thing. I'd rather be doing this." Performing on stage, traveling around the great U.S. of A., visiting different cities, and touring with five hot and talented boys is the perfect job. "I need to sing and love to travel. I love being on the road and touring."

Everyone's got an embarrassing moment and Britney is no different. While on tour, one of the members in B*witched had a birthday. During one of the performances someone accidentally left a cupcake on stage. Guess whose dancing feet were first to step in it. "I stepped on the cupcake and slipped and fell." Dancer TJ came to her rescue. He got it off stage and helped the fair maiden up. Britney recovered quickly, still, it was embarrassing "and funny." Britney's an all-around, good-natured pro even at 17.

Let's Hear It for the Boys

Since Justin and JC knew each other from their Mouseketeer days, it took hardly any effort for the two to reunite, especially when they found themselves in Nashville at the same time working with the same vocal coach and writers. How's that for coincidence? The former 'teers really know the meaning behind the Disney song "It's a Small World" firsthand. Even though they had this musical connection, they were working on separate solo projects. Life was a little lonely and uneventful; the projects just weren't exciting enough. Each was going bonkers with no real place to sing, dance, or act. They needed an outlet, and needed one fast. But what are two cute, talented boys to do? The duo had been recording demos for about three months when they got THE CALL from Chris: Want to form a group? As Justin puts it, "It was Fate." Cut to member number four. Chris was already working with New Yorker Joey Fatone at Orlando's Universal Studios. When the four got together for the first time, it was an instant good vibe. Soon the four could be spotted at clubs dancing up a storm, where their slick hip-hop moves had everyone wanting to know what group they were in. Inspired by the massive praise from onlookers, the quartet decided to form a band and started looking for a bass voice. Justin's old vocal coach from Tennessee knew the perfect match to turn four into five. Clinton, Mississippi, crooner James Lance had the ultimate look, moves, and of course, sound. He was still in school and was class president at the time he met up with the guys. At first he wasn't sure if they were serious, but after a second meeting, he knew they were. Ironically, Lance had originally thought his stardom would be found in the sky. He wanted to be an astronaut and had just passed his NASA exam when the boys asked him to move to Orlando. He said yes, and bingo—a band was formed. As with Britney, it didn't take long for them to become a huge pop success. But it didn't happen as quickly as it did for Britney. "We'd perform for whoever would listen," Justin shares with *Entertainment Weekly*. "We'd be in the middle of a restaurant saying, 'Can we sing for you?'" Life fell into the fast lane when the five singers hooked up with their current managers, Jonny Wright and Lou Pearlman. Within months the boys were gearing up and ready to record their first album, titled *'N Sync*. Then it was off to try the band out in Europe. Almost as soon as their music was released, it started to climb the charts. Opening for Janet Jackson during her Velvet Rope tour pushed them into the spotlight and onto the fame train, where they have had themselves a fast and wonderful ride.

Each artist is a show-business veteran, making the group a conglomerate of talented singers and dancers; each has studied under the same choreographer who's worked with Prince and Michael Jackson. As wholesome as Britney and sweet as apple pie, these guys have no bad raps. Who ever said "nice guys finish last" certainly didn't know the fellas of 'N Sync.

Justin Randall Timberlake

Called the "boy wonder" at 18, Justin is still considered the baby in this group, and the most talented. "I've been singing since I was two," claims Justin to *Teen People.* "If I could talk, I could sing." Like Britney, he was always performing. At 13 Justin left MMC to go back to school, and like Britney, was soooo bored. The classroom was definitely not for him. "I didn't have the inspiration that music gave me, and it hit me: That's my place in the world. That's where I belong," admits Justin in a recent interview.

Originally from Memphis, Justin is a big, big basketball fan and player. "I love basketball and whenever I've the chance, I play like crazy. I'm also a bit of a shopaholic, and collect North Carolina basketball gear."

Perhaps Britney and Justin really are soulmates: Aside from their close ages, they both share the

Mickey Mouse Club, a love for music, and a favorite color (baby blue), and both of their moms are named Lynn. Coincidence? I think not. Justin's heroes, on the other hand, are more athletic-oriented. He'd love to have a one-on-one game with his idol, the recently retired Michael Jordan. "I'd start off by asking him why he quit basketball and well, we'd just carry on from there," he tells one reporter.

Fun Stats

Favorite food: "I love cereal. I've a huge Tupperware bowl almost full of it. I like Apple Jacks," he announces in a recent interview. "When we go to a restaurant for breakfast I take all the cereal. I don't eat a lot of chocolate, I prefer healthy food."

Code name: Mr. Smooth. Why? "The guys call me Mr. Smooth 'cause I went to buy a suit while I was in England. But I'm really athletic so I've got loads of sportswear, too—including 20 pairs of sneakers!" he admits to a reporter.

Most prized possession: His voice.

Favorite word: Crunk. It means crazy.

Christopher Alan Kirkpatrick

The one with the sense of humor, a love for gags and silly jokes, Chris is called ''the prankster'' by some. Yet, at 27, Chris plays the Dad role too since he's the oldest. Born in Pennsylvania, he now lives in Orlando with JC, Justin, and his mother. ''I'm the eldest—and most hyper member. I need lots of calming down!'' he admits in an interview. As a child, he dreamed of being the next Gene Kelly, but it was a singing gig where he sang old Fifties-style doo-wop songs that gave him the idea to form 'N Sync. Chris is really specific about what he likes and the things he doesn't. The beach is one of his favorite places and he lives near one. He loves writing and listening to music. Because of his short attention span, the singer says he gets bored easily, a trait he hates. Even though he's a comedian, he can also be very deep and sentimental. His biggest musical influences are his comrades. ''I'd have to say it was the rest of the band,'' Chris says sweetly during an interview. ''I know how hard they work and their reasons for doing it. I just think they're incredible. Michael Jackson is my most famous influence, though.'' The best thing, he says, about being in a band is that he gets to see his musical ideas come to life. Now *that's* cool.

Fun Stats

Favorite food: Tacos, pizza.
Worst memory: The death of his father.
Prized possession: His Rollerblades and surf-board.
Family details: Four half-sisters, Molly, Kate, Emily, and Taylor.
Code name: Crazy. Why? "I'm quite hyper," he says in a recent interview.
Favorite word: Dude.
A Chris secret: He wears glasses sometimes.

Joseph Anthony Fatone Jr.

Born in Brooklyn, New York, 22-year-old Joey moved to Orlando when he was six with his parents, brother Steve, and sister Janine. A true Superman fan—though some might consider Joey a superhero of sorts—he collects Superman memorabilia. That includes T-shirts, jewelry, lunch boxes . . . anything and everything. A natural-born clubhopper, as a kid Joey could be found ripping up the dance floor late into the evenings.

"The thing I hate most of all is fake people," he boldly shares with a reporter. His biggest musical influence was his dad. "He used to sing in a group called the Orions. They weren't famous but they were great. He listened to a lot of older, Fifties music, and that's what first influenced me,'' he shares in a recent article. Like Britney, Joey feels traveling is the best part of being in a band. He, too, loves visiting different places, London being one of his favorites. ''There's a real buzz about the city,'' he adds. Before joining the band, Joey did some film work. He had small roles in two movies, *Once Upon A Time In America* and *Matinee*, and appeared on the TV series *Sea Quest.* Joey is most comfortable on stage, ''Or in front of the camera. No matter what I do, I go at it full-tilt and can't be stopped.''

Fun Stats

Favorite food: ''I'm Italian so I love lasagna and anything Italian, especially home-cooked food. There are very few restaurants that are as good as my mom's cooking,'' he announces in a recent interview.

Code name: Mr. Flirt. Why? ''I'm always happy. I'm the most flirtatious and the happy-go-lucky one in the band,'' he shares with a reporter. ''If someone's down I try to get them in a good mood—that's my charm! I've got to look on the bright side of everything.''

Favorite word: Burrtt!

Favorite item of clothing: His Superman T-shirt.
Favorite author: Shakespeare. "He was brilliant. I'd like to know what he was thinking about when he came up with the plays."
Favorite activity: Aside from performing—flirting.

James Lance Bass

Born in Laurel, Mississippi, Lance lives in Orlando with his parents, about a mile away from his band buddies. He has one sibling, 23-year-old sister Stacey. "The guys call me Scoop, 'cause when they ask me about our itinerary, I always know!" he admits in a recent interview. His likes and dislikes are simple. "I love the beach. In fact I'm the biggest beach bum and have the legs to prove it—my hairs are bleached blond! But I like the more adventurous stuff like rock climbing and skydiving," he tells a reporter. His biggest musical influence is American country singer, Garth Brooks. "I'm not really into country and western, and I don't own a hat or boots, but he's just a really interesting guy. His shows are wonderful," he adds. For Lance, the best thing about being in a band is the chance to be on a stage and performing. And like Britney, he loves to see his fans, family, and friends in the audience and the enjoyment they get from his music. When he isn't doing 'N Sync stuff, he manages two up-and-coming county artists, Meredith Edwards and Jack Defeo. How he fits it all into his busy schedule is a mystery to his fellow band members. "In school, I had to do everything. I was the president of this, president of that, in this club, in that. Student Council. Honor Society. Plus, I had two jobs," he tells *Teen People*. From day one, Lance knew the band would work out well. "The first time we sang together, I was, like, 'This is it,' " he states in an article. He, too, is a big Shakespeare fan, and like Joey, would be ecstatic to have a one-on-one with the prolific writer. "I'd want to know if he really wrote that stuff, and if he actually thought his writing was as great as it is," he says in a recent article.

Fun Stats

Favorite food: "I love French toast! When you dip bread in egg yolk and then fry it, it's delicious," he admits in an article. "I was so pleased when I was in Europe, because that's what they have for breakfast!"

Code name: Mr. Cool. Why? "I'm generally laid-back, because I don't really care about anything. I hate my hair. I only take about two minutes getting ready, because I'm not so bothered with how I look," he tells a reporter.

Family business: He has a management company named Free Lance Entertainment.

Joshua Scott Chasez (JC)

At 22, JC may not be the youngest, but he's the most laid-back. Originally from Washington, D.C., he now lives in Orlando with two of the band members. As one can guess, he's totally into singing, dancing, and writing music. "I love the movies and anything that keeps me fit, especially in-line skating," he tells one reporter. "We do it all the time." His biggest musical influences are Sting and Seal: "They're brilliant writers." Since his MMC days, what might have changed? As Britney says, he's matured. What hasn't changed is his respect and love for the people around him. "The best thing about being in a band is the friendship. Having people around you so you're never lonely," he shares in an interview. When he was asked who'd he'd like to have a one-on-one with, his answer was a pretty religious one: Jesus Christ. A lover of naps, his comrades sometimes call him "Mr. Sleepy." On stage, of course, he's just the opposite: wide-eyed and totally energized. Like Britney, JC is very hard on himself, and the group. "If we make a mistake on stage," he confides to *Teen People*, "I'm the one who says 'Let's really work on that.' But that's because I see the potential of this group."

Fun Stats

Favorite food: "I love Chinese food. Even when we're on tour I try to have it at least once a week," he admits in a recent article.

Most prized possession: His Hard Rock Cafe menu collection.

A JC secret: "Usually I keep a stuffed animal from a show to sleep on while we're traveling," he admits to a reporter. Isn't that sweet?

Code name: Mr. Casual. Why? Not into prepping for a date, he'll "wear whatever's in the closet. I like casual clothes. That's what I feel comfortable in, and that's important when you're on a date," he says in an interview.

Biggest turnoff: People who lie.

Family details: A 17-year-old brother, Tyler, and 20-year-old sister, Heather.

As of now, 'N Sync is recording its third album in Burbank, California, with Grammy-winning songwriter Diane Warren, (she wrote "How Do I Live Without You") and Celine Dion's producer, Guy Roche. "We're a family just like any other perfectly dysfunctional family," JC says openly to *Hit Sensation*. "We're always around each other, but as long as we respect each other's boundaries and give each other space, it all runs smoothly."

That's just one of the reasons why 'N Sync works so well together. Others are equal partnership, understanding, and a common bond. "We're all into what we do," says JC in a recent article. "We all love to sing, dance, write. Do whatever we can to entertain. That's what we share." Clearly these criteria are the glue that holds the group together. The way JC feels, it's more like cement.

Glue isn't the only thing that sticks to 'N Sync. Their fans, die-hard teens, are pretty attached. Why is that? Chris has the answer. "We're the first group to throw in their face hardcore dancing and singing, then sing a pretty ballad on stools, then (get) right back in their face dancing again," Chris tells *Teen People*. "This has never been about fame or money to us," he continues. "It's always about entertaining."

Don't ask Britney to pick favorites, she claims she loves them all the same. But she recently told AOL that her favorite 'N Sync-er was Lance. Hmmm . . . very interesting.

The way they all got together was definitely a result of good karma. Fate has brought the three Mouseketeers together again and has introduced Britney to some very charming and lovable guys. One could say that they've worked well together on TV. Now years later, performing on stage, the six are totally in sync.

These days, guys share more than a stage with their girl-pal Britney. Jonny Wright, their manager just came aboard the Spears' team. "I saw how talented Britney was, but I also saw there was more development needed," he tells *Entertainment Weekly*. Though everyone's titles are still evolving, "Larry's the manager, and Jonny's the co-manager," says Britney to *Entertainment Weekly*. "Or maybe it's the other way around. I'm not sure but it works out really well." Yes, it does.

10

Britney Sightings

It seems like anywhere you look, whoop—there she is. Since she started touring, there have been tons of Britney sightings. From her new Tommy Hilfiger ads to the daytime TV talkshow circuit, Britney's face is making the rounds. There have also been endless radio interviews and music specials, some of which have appeared on MTV and VH-1. Aside from a mall appearance or two, she's been in almost every major magazine. She has had articles about her in all the cool places one would expect, *Disney Adventure*, *Teen Beat*, *People*, *Girl's Life*, *Billboard*, *Entertainment weekly*, *Teen Celebrity*, *Newsweek*, and *Time*, to name a few. She's also given mega interviews online, as well. And that's just the beginning. There are over 4,500 Websites, she's just signed a modeling contract with Company Modeling Management, and she's supposed to shoot a McDonald's commercial with Grant Hill. Yeah, I'll take fries with that.

Looking pretty in pink at the 1999
American Music Awards.

(Paul Fenton/Shooting Star)

Britney flashes her famous smile
for the camera.

(Mary Monaco/Shooting Star)

Hanging out backstage, waiting for the curtain to open and the fans to go wild.

(Mary Monaco/Shooting Star)

Promoting her single
"Baby One More Time" in London.

(Mark Allan/Globe Photos, Inc.)

With her girl-next-door good looks,
Britney's a fashion icon for
teenage girls everywhere.

Britney added some star power
to *Teen People*'s first
anniversary party.

London calling.
Britney hit the road to promote
"Baby One More Time" overseas.

(Mark Allan/Globe Photos, Inc.)

The camera loves her,
her fans adore her—Britney is the girl
who has it all.

(Ernie Paniccioli/Retna Ltd., USA)

Dawson's Creek

Yes, you too have heard all the talk about Britney's appearances on the WB's hit show *Dawson's Creek*. In fact, her upcoming acting gig has generated as much publicity and talk as her CD. Here's the story thus far. Though no official dates have been set because of her knee injury and the lost time of shooting her next video, she will most probably start taping next season, in the new millennium. She's supposed to shoot three episodes, but one never knows. Britney could become a regular. Will she have a little fling with Pacey? Will she swap gossip with Joey? Expectations are high, but no one knows the plot just yet, not even Britney. Though it would be kind of cool if she could kiss Dawson, even if it's just one quick peck.

Shot on location in Wilmington, North Carolina, the hour-long drama focuses on the relationships of four high school sophomores growing up in Capeside, a small coastal town in Massachusetts. The main players are Dawson Leary and his friends Joey, Jen, and Pacey. Created by *Scream*'s Kevin Williamson, the show has quickly become the highest-rated series in the history of the WB network.

James Van Der Beek: Dawson Leary

Twenty-year-old James is a happy camper. Dedication and talent helped land him the juicy leading role in *Dawson's Creek,* but it was a knock on the head that led him to acting. When he was 13, a mild concussion had him on the bench that year rather than the football field. So instead of sitting on the sidelines, he decided to try out for the school play and landed the lead role of Danny Zuko in the school's production of *Grease.* James did children's theater in his hometown of Cheshire, Connecticut, but realized he needed more than that to be happy and to stretch his acting range.

At 16, he was still theater-obsessed, so his mother agreed that for one summer he could travel the three hours each way into New York City in order to pursue acting professionally. While he landed an agent and a manager on his very first visit, he didn't find much success auditioning for commercials. The next year he was cast in the Off-Broadway play *Finding the Sun.* This was a defining experience for him as an actor, and he commuted six hours every day during the limited three-month run for rehearsals and performances, in the middle of high school. Wow—that's a lot of hours and a ton of commitment. After that experience, he starred in *Shenandoah* at the Goodspeed Opera House. It wasn't long before he found his new home on the set of WB and the rest is history. His film work includes *I Love You, I Love You Not*, which co-stars Clare Danes, *Angus* (he played the school jock who torments an overweight teen), *Harvest* and the box-office smash *Varsity Blues*. Don't you think he and Britney would make a cute couple? Even if it's just a quick thing?

Katie Holmes: Joey Potter

Katie Holmes is pretty, lovable, and captivating. She's also one of the hottest newcomers to enter the acting business. Like Britney, she landed major roles in both films and TV in a very short time. Born and raised in Toledo, Ohio, she started acting in theater productions in high school, but didn't think she had a shot at stardom since she lived in the Midwest. Her big break came during a national modeling and talent convention in New York City. She hooked up with a talent manager who suggested she come to Los Angeles for television's pilot season. On her very first audition, Katie dazzled the casting director for the feature film *The Ice Storm* (she plays Libbets Casey, Tobey Maguire's love interest). The film won the screenplay award at the Cannes Film Festival and gave Katie's acting career a real boost. Talk about beginner's luck! When the next pilot season came up during her senior year of high school, Katie opted to skip coming out to Los Angeles so she could perform in her school's production of *Damn Yankees* as Lola. For the *Dawson's Creek* audition, she sent in a videotape from Toledo, and when the callback conflicted with her play's opening night, she declined rather than let down her classmates—that's one devoted student. Blown away by her commitment to her peers, the producers rescheduled her audition. After securing the part of Joey Potter and graduating from high school, Katie relocated to Wilmington, North Carolina, and began taping the show. Writer Kevin Williamson was so impressed with her portrayal of his character that he cast her in his upcoming movie *Killing Mrs. Tingle*. She can also be seen in *Disturbing Behavior* and *Go*, which stars Jay Mohr and Scott Wolf. Katie and Britney would definitely hit it off. They'd make cool friends.

Michelle Williams: Jennifer Lindley

This is Michelle's first starring role in a TV series, but unlike her fellow cast members, she had already starred in many feature films. Like Katie and Britney, Michelle is a small-town girl, born and raised in rural Kalispell, Montana, before moving with her family to San Diego when she was ten years old. She became involved in community theater productions and was soon commuting to Los Angeles for professional auditions. At age 14, Michelle made her big-screen splash in the 1994 family film *Lassie*. Trust us, she was no dog. After that, she filmed *Species*, *A Thousand Acres*, starring Michelle Pfeiffer and Jennifer Jason Leigh, and *Halloween H20*. This time Michael Myers was back, with a vengeance—and so was Michelle's film career. Look for her in the upcoming movie *Dick*, with Kirsten Dunst.

Joshua Jackson: Pacey Witter

Joshua Jackson may play a rambunctious and free-spirited adolescent grasping for adulthood, but in real life he's a hard-working, focused, and determined actor. His first-season storyline, which involved a romantic affair with his teacher, caught the attention of just about everyone, and thus a TV/film career was made. But Josh had been working in the acting world for a large chunk of his life. A native of Vancouver, British Columbia, he landed his first professional acting gig at age nine, a commercial for British Columbia Television. This led to a part on the TV series *MacGyver,* which helped him secure the lead role of Charlie in a Seattle-based musical production of *Willy Wonka and the Chocolate Factory*. Like

Britney, Josh also joined the Disney family. His induction happened when he signed on to shoot all three *Mighty Ducks* movies. His most recent work has been in *Apt Pupil*, starring Ian Mc-Kellen; *Urban Legend,* and *Cruel Intentions* with Ryan Phillippe and Sarah Michelle Gellar. These films have helped to make him a box office success. Currently, Joshua and his family divide their time between Vancouver and California. He, too, would be a good match for bubble-pop-star Britney.

11

You Go, Girl

Chart Breaker

If 1998 was the year of the boy bands—BSB, 'N Sync, Hi-Five—then this is the year of the chicks. Coming off the tails of Spice Girl-mania, B*witched, Cleopatra, and Lauryn Hill have made lots of musical noise. In February, for only the second time in music history, three women, Britney being one of them, held the top three songs at the same time. Monica's "Angel of Mine," Brandy's "Have You Ever?," and Britney's ". . . Baby One More Time." The only other time there have been three hot tunes by female artists in the top three spots was in 1990: "Escapade" by Michael Jackson's little sister Janet, "Black Velvet" by Alannah Myles (anyone know where she went?), and "Love Will Lead You Back" by Taylor Dayne (desperately looking for her career). Britney is one of the youngest of the six women included in this special category. Who says age matters?

Though the 'N Sync tour ended in January, Britney's career was just beginning. After her single and CD were released, Britney's music and ratings won her all sorts of titles. She was the first new female artist to have a simultaneous Number 1 single in the Hot 100 and Number 1 album on the Billboard 200. She was the first new artist, male or female, to jump into the Number 1 spot on both the Hot 100 and Billboard 200. And the awards didn't stop there. She was also the first new artist to have a single go to the Number 1 spot the same week that the album debuted at Number 1 on the Billboard 200. In Europe, news came from abroad that so many people wanted her work that Jive Records had to make extra copies of the single to keep up with the demand. It was reported that over 300,000 copies were sold by Thursday night. Britney's single sold more in the first day it was released than Lenny Kravitz's record "I'll Fly Away" did in one week. That's rather amazing for a new kid whose name was just being introduced to Europe. "I'm so pleased my British fans like my record." Britney tells the *Scottish Daily*. "It really means a lot to me." Even though Britney has been to London only once before, she has already built a huge following. FYI: Her album also hit Number 1 on the Canadian SoundScan chart.

Heart Breaker

Okay people, just for the record—let's clear something up once and for all, and move on, shall we? Britney and Justin are *just friends*. Once more for the disbelievers—according to Britney, they're just good buds. "No, it's not true," she insists to an interviewer regarding the rumors. The members of 'N Sync are like brothers to her—not dating material.

"Me and Britney?" Justin tells *MTV News* online. "Sorry." Joey also got in on the act in the same interview. "I'm actually dating Britney. We've been together for seven years," he says, kidding around. Of course Lance didn't miss the opportunity to crack a joke and add fuel to the fire. "I'm dating Britney and two of her dancers," he chuckles.

Even though Britney has claimed there are no sparks, it's easy to see why the rumor got started in the first place. Britney's first kiss was received by none other than Justin. And just to dispel any others, she and Nick Carter are not going out either: "We're just labelmates." (Both are signed with Jive.) They went out for a while but that is it! Really!

She's been described as sexy and hot, but Britney considers herself to be honest, trustworthy, and "just a sweet girl that anyone can talk to." It's no wonder she's in major demand. People just can't stop talking about the teen sensation. These days, Britney is breaking a lot of hearts, but not because she's dating—she isn't. "I really don't have the time," she admits to the *Star Tribune.* "I know that sounds selfish, but it would probably be more selfish if I tried to keep a boyfriend. I had a boyfriend when I started this job, but he didn't quite understand everything I was going through." The boy was Reggie Jones, and he was her first real love. "He was a senior when she was a freshman," shares Robbey, an old classmate of Britney's. The two went out for a few years, but Reggie was a hometown guy and, according to Britney, rather "possessive, and too jealous." He was always worried about what she was doing and never gave her a chance to breathe. Eventually she just wanted to be left alone. Because she's on the road so much, Britney insists there must be a ton of trust between two people for any relationship to work. "I'm young and I just want to have fun right now," Britney insists to a reviewer. But rumor has it she is dating someone. Who this mystery man is, no one knows. But he's a lucky guy to have captured the princess's heart. It's still to early too tell if he's a keeper or if he's "the one." Either way, chances are, he's a hottie." A guy that has a wonderful personality and can make me laugh and has a lot of confidence, I find very sexy,'' she says.

Though she hasn't been dating up a storm like most teens her age, her songs however, tell another story. ''. . . Baby One More Time,'' is all about feelings and emotions, the joy and pain of being in love, and the head-over-heels, all-out gushing joy of being with someone special. ''My songs,'' she tells the *Star Tribune*, ''even though I've not necessarily felt all those emotions, most of the girls my age can relate to maybe wanting to feel that way at some point.'' And she's right. She has a real instinctual connection to her music and to her listeners.

12

A Twist of a Knee

With every bit of sun, a little rain must fall. And on February 12, it fell hard. Actually, it wasn't rain that fell—rather it was Britney doing the slipping. During a rehearsal for her upcoming video, she fell and dislocated her knee. The only other time Britney had had a bad injury like this was during her old gymnastics days. When she was eight or so, she hurt herself pretty badly while doing a routine. Still, no one likes to be in pain and this couldn't have come at a worse time. It meant canceling the *Tonight Show with Jay Leno* and the Grammy Awards. Britney was inconsolable. This major setback also postponed her July dance rehearsals for her own music tour, which was supposed to happen in midsummer. In March, she had some surgery on her knee. At the Doctors Hospital in New Orleans, Dr. Tim Finney supposedly removed a one-inch piece of loose cartilage—ouch, that must've hurt. But Britney is a trouper and recovered really quickly. "When my leg gets better, which will probably be in three or four more weeks, and I'm able to dance on my leg again, I'll do my second video, for 'Sometimes.'' And there will be more dancing in it than '. . . Baby One More Time.' Even though it's a mid-tempo song, there is brilliant choreography and it's really out there and so that is why my leg HAS to be better!'' she tells AOL. ''I don't have a cast on my leg. I have nothing on it actually. I have butterfly stitches because they just went in with a scope and didn't have to really cut me. They had to clean out the chips of bones that were in my knee.'' Working with a physical therapist helped get her knee back into shape and her confidence back on track. Not one for sitting around, the bouncy singer will be dancing up a storm and ready to work in no time. ''I need to practice my dancing every day, but I don't, and when I don't it makes me out of shape and then when I start dancing again I hurt my leg like I did. I hadn't danced in . . . I don't know how long and I go, and like a goof, twist my knee!'' she tells an interviewer. What has come out of this experience is how concerned her friends and fans have been. That's really helped Britney feel loved, and made her want to get better faster. ''I want to thank my wonderful fans and all the people who have offered their love and support,'' she says to *Entertainment Wire.*

Her plans for her own tour are still in deep development. There is talk of her breaking into international waters as soon as her knee heals and she finishes shooting her second video, "Sometimes." Canada, where her album was released, will be the first stop. Gigs and performances in Germany, France, the UK, and Asia have also been penciled in. Knowing Britney, she'll have her bags packed long before any dates are secured.

13

That's a Wrap

Road Work Ahead

Life on the road can be hard. Britney misses her friends and family often, and though speaking to them constantly is a help, it's not quite the same as opening your door, stepping outside, and waving across the road to your cousin, or shouting across the street to a friend. Or even getting up, walking into the kitchen, and having breakfast with your kid sister. Britney's whole life has changed—she's gone from a small-town southern gal to a sharp-shooting woman of the world.

A little on the reserved side, Britney was never a screaming fan herself. Sure, she'd put pictures and posters up on her wall and in her locker of her favorite stars and guys she thought were cute, but she wasn't the type to go crazy and scream. Of course, that hasn't stopped her fans from sharing their excitement or vocalizing their hellos. Sometimes fan appreciation can get a little OOC—

Out of Control. Sometimes the star is just bombarded by fans who all want to talk, touch, and get an autograph. "They're like, crazy," she says to *Entertainment Weekly*. "It's flattering to a certain extent, but sometimes they get a little bit overbearing." Jonny Wright, her new manager, understands the situation totally. "Here's a girl who basically went from nowhere to Number 1 overnight," he explains to *Entertainment Weekly*. "The Backstreet Boys and 'N Sync had time to develop, to work on performing and the press before all the pressure came down. What's going on with Britney right now is she's just getting bombarded." Even though the pop princess loves what's she's doing, she does have some fears—and rightly so. They involve the standard: The need to watch your back, how fame can change a person, the danger of getting a swelled head. "Losing my identity and privacy" is probably her biggest concern, she tells *Teen Celebrity*. "How fun can it be going out with your friends when your bodyguard is right there all the time?" she adds. She's also noticed people staring at her, which makes her a tad uncomfortable, to say the least. "That's a little weird."

Unwanted intruders and crazed fans also fall into the overwhelming category. Recently, an unexpected and uninvited guest showed up on her doorstep. He parked his car a block or so away from her house, then walked casually over. "Girls scream, but boys, when they're a major fan of yours, are freaky,'' says Britney to *People* magazine. Luckily, her mom was home. Still, the situation was terribly unsettling and caused quite a stir. Other concerns? Britney worries a lot, too. ''I'll be in bed at night,'' she admits during an interview, ''and I'll just think of the stupidest things. I'm so paranoid.'' Understandably so. Some of her underwater feeling is from living in a tiny community. Used to small groups of people, all of whom she knows on a first-name basis, a laid-back lifestyle, and family that surround her, all of this must seem surreal and scary. Britney often misses the comforts of home, the familiar smell of fresh-cut grass, the simplicity of country life. Growing up in a small town does have its share of positives. Gramma and Grampa are literally just around the corner and, Britney says, will cook any fruity pie you might desire. On a bad note, though, everyone knows everyone's business. Small towns talk, and they talk loudly. ''When I come home, I kind of have to keep it a secret. A low profile,'' she confides to *MTV News*. ''I really don't tell anybody I'm coming home 'cause if I did, I'd have to go visit nine million people.'' But that doesn't stop the star from making a cameo appearance. Britney recently went back home hoping to kick off her dancing shoes and settle into her old roots. That doesn't mean fame doesn't have its own rewards. Anyone will tell you it's great. And this gal wouldn't give it up for anything in the world. Being recognized does have its advantages. "The best is getting free stuff like ice cream" and clothing, she admits to *Teen Celebrity*.

Home Again

If the old saying "Home is where the heart is" rings true, it's also where the bed is. "I love my bed," claims Britney to one reporter. "I'm such a homey person, I have everything where it's supposed to be. I love going into my room." So does someone else. Like the star herself, her room is in demand. Britney's sister, Jamie Lynn, has taken over in a big way. If she can't have her older sis, then commandeering her room is probably the next best thing. Besides, who wouldn't want to be surrounded by all those dolls? Yes, you heard right—Britney's room is filled with dolls. She's obsessed with them. Aside from having the best voice in Kentwood, she's probably got the most amazing doll collection, too. In fact, she gets a new one each Christmas. "The best present I ever got was probably my collector doll," she tells AOL. "She's so pretty and looks like an older woman that had a hat on and reminded me of my grandmother." Rumor has it her bedroom is filled to the gills with dolls from all over the country.

They are everywhere, perched on her desk, propped up against the window sill, and covering her bed. "Every time I come home, I'm like 'Ahem!' because all my dolls are put somewhere different and I'm just like . . . ugh! I'm such a clean nut," she says in regards to her sister's take-over.

Britney's kid sis is also showing signs of joining the singing brigade. Britney says Jamie Lynn can really belt out a song, too. Both are said to come across as shy when you first meet them. Shy? Our singing diva? It's hard to believe, almost impossible, but many local folks and friends of the family recall Britney as being shy. "She really was," Mrs. Hughes, Britney's old teacher confides. "But when she got on stage and was in front of a microphone, she came alive. She just lit up like a 1,000-watt bulb." Britney herself has admitted to this. Hard to believe, but when she was younger, she was quiet and timid. "My little sister, she's such a spitfire, there's no telling what she'll do. When I was younger I was shy and soft-spoken, but not her. She can sing really well." Shyness, of course, cannot be said for her now—actually for neither of the Spears girls anymore. Britney performs in front of thousands of screaming, elated teens, and Jamie Lynn has a bit of a wild side. Britney says she's full of personality. Sometimes, there's just no stopping the kid or figuring out what her next move is going to be. Jamie

Lynn is following in her sister's footsteps by doing some modeling for clothing catalogs, too. Perhaps Tommy Hilfiger will use both Spears girls for his next big spread.

Concert at Home

Usually Kentwood is rather quiet. And if you didn't know different, you might think you've entered a time warp. When Britney stopped in her hometown before opening for 'N Sync in Baton Rouge, the town came alive. In the distance the loud sounds of horns could be heard. The closer you got the louder the cheering became. There were banners with "WE LOVE YOU BRITNEY" written on them, balloons, and fans screaming in appreciation and excitement. Everyone in town was waiting to welcome home their pride and joy. (Okay, so it might not have been that dramatic—still, it was pretty intense.)

"In Kentwood Plaza, stores had signs out, and everyone was incredibly supportive and excited," shares Mrs. Hughes, who cried at the concert because she was so proud of her prize student. "People wrote things all over car windows, it was like a pep rally. Then we followed her to Baton Rouge for the concert. We had a tailgating party outside. Everyone had a wonderful time."

Class Photo

Now that Kentwood is becoming famous for the 17-year-old prodigy, VH-1, MTV, and *People* magazine have all made personal housecalls. Most recently, *Rolling Stone* magazine came to Britney's alma mater to do a huge photo shoot. "The school was just total chaos, because everyone wanted to see her," explains Mrs. Hughes. "There are enough of us teachers here who remember her and tell stories about her, so many of our students feel as though they have an inside scoop."

Still caring for her knee, Britney showed up with a brace on, but the true professional didn't let a little pain stop her from joining in the festivities. As you can imagine, Britney wasn't the only one ready for her close-up. Everybody in the fifth grade had her hair parted and braided just like Britney's. Some eighth graders paraded around in the same school uniform she wears in the video. They looked like little Britney-ettes. One student wrote "I LOVE BRITNEY SPEARS" on his chest—now *that's* loyalty.

Help

This question gets asked a lot. Fans write for guidance, people approach her in need of suggestions, and interviewers ask what advice she can offer to other aspiring singers. The career path is always a hard one; as with anything, Britney always offers advice that's helpful and optimistic, but mostly, realistic. "Just believe and work hard," says the superstar to AOL's Entertainment Asylum. "It takes time. I'm 17 now, and I've been doing it all my life." She also adds, "Make as many contacts as you can and follow your dreams." If you follow her trip, that's pretty true. From her first church appearance to her own soon-to-be announced personal tour, Britney has been performing on and off the stage for all of her life. "If you have a love for singing and dancing, go for it, because God's given you a talent and you should express it and use it. Go for your dreams and what you believe in and stay confident and happy with yourself."

Coming to a Close

Britney is loving New York and is quickly becoming a die-hard fan of the big city. Still, she's a

Southern girl. You can take the girl out of the South, but you can't take the South out of Britney. Polite and respectful, Britney is often quoted as saying "Yes, sir" and "Yes, ma'am," or "It's a Southern thing."

As for college, Britney has decided to put it on hold, though she does want to go. "I definitely want something to fall back on and to have something to look forward to," says the star to a reporter. "This business is so crazy." Actually, Britney *is* in college, sort of: the school of life, and she's getting all A's. "I think of this as my college right now, being away from home, traveling and visiting so many different places. I just want to see the world." Britney's efforts will be to focus on her singing career and do some film work. Now that she's mastered the music industry, this news of TV and film gigs comes as no shock. Her ideal role? "Something where I could also sing and dance. And I want my co-star to be Brad Pitt or Ben Affleck." Wouldn't we all? Britney's not asking for too much!

In a recent article on Britney, a writer from the *Houston Chronicle* asked that age-old question: whether "she can build a career or if she will simply end up as one more face on the teen-idol totem pole." Silly writer, not a chance. Britney Spears isn't going anywhere but up. "I want to be an artist everyone can relate to." Britney says in *Just Nikki*. "I want to have a few records behind me and keep building and building." She swears to *MTV News*, "I want to grow as a person each time an album comes out. Music will always remain my main priority. I want music to be part of my life."

As for her leg—well, that was probably a much-needed break (no pun intended). "Right now with my leg I'm totally slowing down, but it's good because I needed the time off. Things do get crazy, but I'm about to go insane right now because I'm used to being so busy. I get to go home and see my friends about every four weeks. So I get to be pretty normal," she says.

Today, Britney lives in an apartment owned by Jive and has completed the tenth grade through correspondence courses from the University of Nebraska. Still a home girl at heart, she returns to Kentwood for proms, homecoming, and family events. "I know it's not a normal way to be, but it's as normal as I can get," she says honestly to the *Star Tribune*. "I'm still very happy." And that's what's most important. Right? "I love performing more than anything. This is what I've wanted to do all my life," she adds to *Pop* magazine. "It's everything I dreamed it would be, and I've enjoyed every minute of it." So have we.

14

Britney Stats

The Bio

Full name: Britney Jean Spears

Birthdate: December 2, 1981

Astrological sign: Sagittarius

Birthplace: Kentwood, Louisiana

Current residence: New York and Kentwood

Hair color : Brownish-blond

Eye color: Brown

Height : 5'4"

Weight : 105 lbs.

Family: Dad, Jamie, 46; mom, Lynne, 43; brother, Bryan, 21; sister, Jamie Lynn, 8.

Body part she hates most: Her feet—"I have ugly feet."

Hobbies: Singing, dancing, and reading trashy novels

Last book read: *The Horse Whisperer*

Sports activities: Basketball and swimming

What drives her insane? "People who blow sunshine up your butt."

Motto: "Life is short. Don't waste it."

These Are a Few of Her Favorite Things

Favorite Disney character: Goofy

Favorite teams : Chicago Bulls, New York Yankees

Favorite pastime: Shopping

Favorite movies: *My Best Friend's Wedding, Titanic*

Favorite songs: Prince's "Purple Rain", Madonna's "Like a Virgin"

"Favorite artists: Mariah Carey, Michael Jackson, Whitney Houston, Prince, the Backstreet Boys

Favorite actress: Jennifer Aniston

Favorite food : Ice cream (cookie dough flavor)

Favorite colors : Baby blue

Favorite clothing designers: Betsey Johnson, Bebe, A/X by Giorgio Armani

Favorite author: Danielle Steele

Favorite flower: White rose

Favorite cereal: Cocoa Puffs

Hey, What's Your Sign?

Nov. 23–Dec. 21: Sagittarius

Symbol: The archer, a mythic combination of human and horse

Object: Bow and arrow held in mid-arm, ready to release it into the world

Sign: Fire, which stands for creativity

Best day of the week: Thursday

Color: Purple

Gem/stone: Turquoise

Animal: The Horse

Foods: Grapefruits, raisins, and root veggies, and maybe cookie dough ice cream

Best mate: Libra

You couldn't find a better candidate for a typical Sagittarius than Britney. She's so perfect, she could be the Sag poster girl. "Because of the way the planets lined up on the day of Britney's birth, her big emphasis is speed and motion," says renowned New York astrologist Patricia Konigsberg. "Britney is a free spirit, but is also a bit of a control freak. And that will cause her boy trouble in later years."

The way the planets align themselves on different days and at different times all mean something specific to a person who comes into the world at that moment. Like people, no two charts are alike. The stars and planets all help to tell information about ourselves and sometimes even the future.

"Britney has to learn to relax and go with the flow," Patricia continues. "She needs to be physically active and find an outlet which will release all her pent-up animation." That sure sounds like Britney. "She loves to dance and has lots o' energy," adds Patricia. "She hates to be bored." Sags may injure themselves during their activities, but they bounce back and bounce back fast. (There's the injured-knee connection.) Always on the go, Sags often forget to slow down and relax.

Sagittarii are extremely honest, ambitious, and outgoing. Full of self-confidence, they can handle any hardship or challenge life may toss their way. Sags are optimistic from the start; when life throws a Sagittarius a stack of lemons, she doesn't just make lemonade, she makes pitchers of it. And she graciously hands them out to everyone she loves.

Sags are always asking questions and searching for answers. But the archer can get bored easily and is constantly seeking new targets and reaching for higher goals. Sags are natural-born-actors, theatrical folks who will often change their minds at the drop of a hat. They are seekers of everything, and they love a chase. Often rebellious, Sags also have a bit of a temper—so watch out, they're not called the fire sign for nothing. However, they never hold grudges and always forgive and forget. Most important to a Sagittarius is friendship: They are loyal to the end. Fun-loving, open, and warm, it's easy to see why Sags make friends easily. Because they need action and variety, Sags are always on the go and looking for their next big break. Does a music career ring a bell? Sags are never lacking for new hobbies and of course, there's always time for traveling. "On an passionate level," Patricia says, "Britney's a bit of an emotional gal. But she doesn't like to show them."

Because of her sun sign, she's more adventurous and direct. "She's going to have to tone down her mouth," advises Patricia, "because it can get her into trouble."

Sagittarii need to be challenged physically, mentally, and emotionally. Some people tend to think of Sags as airheads but that's only because their minds are going so fast.

Britney's love of travel and her craving for adventure aren't just a coincidence. Sags are restless spirits, mostly because their ruling planet is Jupiter, which can make them itchy and antsy. Ironically, those are two words Britney uses to describe her discontentment. "I want to see the world," she says often in interviews. Sags are natural explorers, and Britney is certainly no different. Many Sags want to help humankind, and they are generous souls who need to share their wealth, knowledge, or talent with others. A person of high values and morals, Sags live in a world of beliefs that good can conquer evil, honesty is best, and life is nothing unless you're doing what makes you happy. Britney has all of these traits, qualities, and more. Seems like the stars and planets have nailed her down to a T.

15

What's in a Name?

William Shakespeare once wrote "What's in a name?" Well, lots! Names tell us our goals, characteristics, and even future. Besides, your parents didn't carefully choose your name for nothing. They did it for a reason. Sometimes people are named after an honored family member, or a favorite star or character, but each name has special meaning to the bearer, and the person who gave it to him or her. Our birth name is part of what makes us different from one another.

Numerology is the study of, you guessed it, numbers—and their meanings. It's based on the belief that the name you were given at birth and the day, month, and year you were born influence who you are and what will happen to you during the course of your lifetime. Like a Magic Eight-ball, it's a little look into the future.

Part of what makes Britney unique is the quirky

individualized spelling of her name. Ironically, it's just two letters different from that of her fave music goddess, Whitney Houston. Substitute the WH for a BR and it's the same. There are several ways Britney's name could have been spelled: Britteny, Brittny, or Brittany. And each would have had a different meaning, characteristic, and future plan. Try each name and see what her life might have turned out like if her name had been spelled differently. First let's try it the way it's spelled:
BRITNEY JEAN SPEARS
Each letter represents a number. Substitute the number with the coinciding letter.

A B C D E F G H I
1 2 3 4 5 6 7 8 9

J K L M N O P Q R
1 2 3 4 5 6 7 8 9

S T U V W X Y Z
1 2 3 4 5 6 7 8

B R I T N E Y   J E A N   S P E A R S
2 9 9 2 5 5 7   1 5 1 5   1 7 5 1 9 1

Now add the numbers together, breaking them down into the lowest possible single digit.
Britney = 2+9+9+2+5+5+7=39,
3+9=12, 1+2=3

Britney Spears

Jean = 1+5+1+5=12, 1+2=3
Spears = 1+7+5+1+9+1=24, 2+4=6
Add them all up 3+3+6=12, 1+2=3
Britney's name number is 3. This is called her destiny number. Now look it up on the chart.

One Destiny: Independent, confident, original, quick, inventive, moral
Two Destiny: Sensitive, supportive, gracious, artistic, a good listener
Three Destiny: Optimistic, creative, dramatic, friendly, winning
Four Destiny: Practical, sensible, honest, serious, hardworking, loyal
Five Destiny: Adventurous, quick, dynamic, sociable, impulsive
Six Destiny: Responsible, caring, artistic, loving, practical, traditional
Seven Destiny: Quiet, refined, intellectual, deep, choosy
Eight Destiny: Powerful, ambitious, confident, conventional, reliable
Nine Destiny: Dreamer, considerate, romantic, sensitive, dynamic, mature

Number three is *so* her. Don't you think? Now try her other possible name spellings and see what she might have been headed for. Then try your name to see what's in your future. While you're at it, compare it to those of your friends, parents, or love interest.

Birthdays hold a similar magic. Let's do Britney's Birthday. It's done the same way you did her name. Britney was born on December 2, 1981. Dec. = 12 (1+2), Day = 2, Year 1981 (1+9+8+1) Now add them all together. 1+2+2+1+9+8+1=24. Than break down 24 into the smallest number. 2+4 = 6. So 6 becomes her birthpath number.

Find Britney's number on the chart, then do yours. See if you guys have the same number or if you'd be compatible as friends. While you're at it, do numbers for your best friend, parents, or siblings as well.

1. Number 1'ers are decisive and courageous. Because you have a lot of energy, you're a natural born leader. A birthpath of 1 of gives greater will power and self-confidence to your personality. On the other hand, because you have so much energy, you're not big on details. You look, but sometimes not as closely as you should. Even though you're sensitive, you sometimes don't show how you feel.

2. Birthpath 2'ers you are emotional, sensitive, artistic and patient. As a 2'er, you're a social but-

terfly who makes friends easily and quickly. In large groups you sometimes get nervous. You are warmhearted and understanding, and often seek affection. Because you're so sensitive, it's hard for you to bounce back when you get upset.

3. Birthpath 3'ers love life! The energy of 3 allows you to bounce back rapidly from setbacks, physical or mental. There is a restlessness in your nature, but you seem to be able to portray an easygoing, sometimes couldn't-care-less attitude. You have a natural ability to express yourself in public, and you always make a very good impression. Because you're so good with words, writing, and speaking you do well in school. A real chatterbox, you love to talk, talk, talk. You are affectionate and loving, but sometimes too sensitive. You are subject to rapid ups and downs.

4. A birthpath number 4 makes you a good manager and organizer. You are responsible, disciplined, sincere, and honest. You are also serious and hard-working. As a 4'er, you sometimes keep things to yourself, and are often stubborn.

5. As a 5 birthpather you work well with people and enjoy them. You are talented, versatile, and very good at presenting ideas. You may have a tendency to get itchy feet at times and need change and travel. You tend to be very progressive, imaginative, and adaptable. Your mind is

quick, clever and analytical. A restlessness in your nature may make you a bit impatient and easily bored with routine. You may have a tendency to shirk responsibility.

6. A birthpath of 6 gives you a responsible, helpful, and understanding nature. Usually you go with your instincts, and because of that, you tend to be open, honest, and very caring with your family and friends.

7. Birthpath 7'ers have a tendency to be perfectionists and that makes you more individualistic in many ways. You can be deep and have good reasoning skills. You are very psychic and sensitive. Always follow your hunches. Since you don't like to take orders, you'd make a better boss. Those with a birthpath of 7 can sometimes be self-centered and a little stubborn.

8. A birthpath of 8 gives you a special gift for business. Your special abilities include conceiving and planning on a grand scale, executive skills, and the ability to judge values. Since you like to be in control, think about starting your own business! You're reliable and trustworthy when it comes to handling money. Idealistic by nature, you are never too busy to spend some time on worthwhile causes, especially if a friend needs you.

9. Birthpath 9'ers are easy to work with, generous,

and totally tolerant. You are always sensitive to others' needs and feelings, and even if the other numbers in your core makeup don't show it, you are very sympathetic and compassionate. As a good friend and listener, you often give more than you get.

For more information about numerology, go on the Web and check out your birthday, love interest, and what your name means. It helps to do a search under ''Numerology and how to.''

16

Fabulous Fans

Some say one's success stems from talent, others claim it's a direct response from industry connections. Then there are the believers who insist that it's from a combination of both. The truth is fame comes from your fans. They can make or break you. You could be more talented then the Beatles and Sheryl Crow put together—if that's possible—but without fan support, you've got nada. Que pasa?

Britney is a true rarity. Not only is she committed to her work, but she thoroughly takes the public and her listeners into account, not something all stars would do. "If it weren't for my fans," she shares with readers in a recent interview with *Zoo Disney*, "no one would listen to my music or buy my records."

She checks her e-mail regularly, too. Who knew? "Felicia, who travels with me," she continues, "carries a laptop with her and we hook it up and look at fan sites."

As if that weren't enough, the busy star has been known to respond to her messages, as well. Here's a letter Britney wrote to her fans in response to their e-mails.

"Dear E-Mailers: Thanks so much for writing to me. I'm trying as hard as I can to return as many letters as possible, but if I haven't gotten to you yet, please know that I am reading your e-mails, and I really appreciate them. It's really cool to get ones from far away places, and from new friends in my home state of Louisiana. Well, I gotta go, cuz the bus is pulling out for the next tour stop, but I wanted to take a minute out to tell you guys thanks again for writing me, and maybe I'll get to meet you somewhere along the tour. Until then, take care, and I'll write again soon. Love, Britney."

Now *this* will blow you away, Britney even went as far as to say she didn't want to play "a mean girl" when asked by a reporter about her upcoming part on *Dawson's Creek*. "I'd want to play a sweet girl, because I wouldn't want to lose any of my fans."

Here are some thoughts and feelings from her loyal listeners. Many were written directly to her; others were found on the Internet, connecting with each other and bonding through common admiration and love for Britney.

And now a word from some important voices—her fans.

"I just wanted to say, I think your song, BABY ONE MORE TIME is one of my favorite songs and a lot of my friends fav, too. We are all so jealous of you (you get to tour with 'N Sync)! You and 'N Sync together in one show must make a really good one!" From: Basketballgirl

"I saw you on Rosie O'Donnell, you and the dancers did great. I can't say you're my favorite singer because I have a lot of favorite singers but I think you have a great voice. Don't listen to those people who say bad stuff about you because they are immature and should think about what they say because they could hurt someone's feelings. Good luck with your career." From: Kristen

"Hey Britney Spears, I'm your biggest Fan. Britney Spears You're so Awesome. I just got your new CD, and I love it. Me and my friends at school are doing your song ". . . Baby One More Time" for a lip sink contest. It's going to be great and I can't wait. I just wanted to let you know that I'm your biggest fan again. And I want to be just like you when I get older." From: Christina

"Tonight is the Super Bowl, you going to watch it? I'm not the biggest football fan but I got to watch it. You are the best thing that has happened to me in a long time. I have dedicated this semester in school to you, so I have to do good. Last semester I really screwed up, I just didn't care. But this time I care, maybe because it is because my parents said that I couldn't go to your concert on May 16th in West Palm Beach with 'N Sync if I didn't make better grades. I cant wait for that, in my mind that is like the BIG DAY for me. I am 17 just like you and feel something for you that just won't go away. Please e-mail my heart, because I e-mail you my heart everyday. Britney good luck in everything you do.'' From: Matt

"Britney I love your song, ''... Baby One More Time.'' I think you should keep up the good work. You are a great singer. You are one of the best singers I know. From your biggest fan.'' From: Whitney

"Britney Spears is a pioneer in the music industry. Her inspirational music will affect artists for years to come. The way she has mastered every field in music including composing, instrumentation, and presentation has no equal. The history of music has not been struck like this since Mozart, making Britney Spears an icon which will never be reproduced. She has a great ass, too.'' From: www.Lothos

"Thank you for being so incredibly cute! Ever since I heard your song and saw your video (which makes my every day) I have not stopped singing it. I love the clothes, voice, looks, and moves, they all get me in a very good mood. Keep on looking good and moving right and I'll keep loving you! Take care. Cheers." From: Thor

"I think your video is really something real nice and I also think it's a shame that we in Holland can't buy your album yet. But when it's here, I will really buy it. In the meantime can you please send me a signed single/album or both, please! I think you're real beautiful. Love your biggest fan." From: Marcel

"Britney is a very good artist and a very nice girl. The music she's making is great. She must go on with the music that she is making right now. I live in the Netherlands and her album is not out yet, but when it is, I will buy it for sure." From: M.Baneman

"Hi. I really think you're hot and this site rocks. You should have larger pic's though. Very good luck in the future!! I love you and your music. I'm a 20-year-old male fan from Sweden." From: lixenz

"Hi, I am a new Britney Spears fan and I think she is awesome. She has a lot of talent. She has a beautiful voice and her dances are so cool. No one can really say they hate her unless they know her personally. Other than that, you anti-Britney people have no reason to hate her. She didn't do anything to you. Please e-mail me or respond to this letter, someone." From: Nikki

"I think Britney Spears is a great singer and role model. I don't think it is right for people who aren't even in the entertainment business to say they hate someone because they sing! I mean look, she made it this far and you Anti-Britney people haven't even gotten started." From: Ashley

"I really like the Backstreet Boys but Britney Spears is so cool! She is totally gorgeous and she can dress the way that I like to dress. She can sing so good and I'm happy that she is the new pop queen because I think that she deserves it with her over the roof and beyond talents to dance and sing! I just love the way that she dances and the moves are so hip and all. To all of the Britney Spears haters out there, I'm sorry but you guys are throwing away the most hip and cool gal singer." From: Fay

"Britney is one of the most pretty girls I ever seen, I saw her my first time on MTV and believe me it was love at first sight. She is the hottest girl I have ever seen. I just got her CD. I am from Guatemala and believe me, we all love you, Britney, because you are the best. I mean you can dance, you can sing, I bet you can do everything I can imagine, and even what I can't. I just Love You Baby." From: Joe

"Oh my god, how can anyone hate Britney? She's pretty, she takes care of herself and her body, she's athletic, she's a good dancer, she could even teach the Backstreet Boys and 'N Sync a move or two, and she can really sing. She has my shoes tap-a-tap-tapping! On top of that, she's a sweet girl with a good head on her shoulders who really wants nothing more than to see the world. What's so wrong about that? For 17, she really inspires young women to fulfill their dreams and do what their heart tells them to do." From: Heather

"Down here in Toronto we love Britney, she was recently here and I got her autograph, the only bad thing is that she was running late, so we couldn't get pictures, nor meet her. She is so beautiful, and me and all my friends would love for her to come down to Toronto again. . . . Best of Luck overseas!" From: Jay

"Britney is the best teen singer I have ever heard or seen. She is down-to-earth, she is nowhere near a snob like many other singers. She is extremely good-looking and can dance very good. She's the best and I totally support her!" From: Sam H.

"Dear Britney Spears: You rock, I give you so much credit for what you have done. You are a solo singer who is only 17 and you are already so famous. I went to Much Music on Friday night. I was at the sound check when you were just practicing, you were awesome in the sound check and the real performance. I hope all goes well in your future years, love one of your fans." From: Robyn

"I think you're the best. I watched you on MMC. I love you and your music. I can't wait till' you come to Las Vegas again. I hope to see you. I also think you're the most attractive person I've ever seen. Keep climbing those charts!!!!" From: James O.

"My interests are playing basketball and football. I like to listen to Mariah Carey and Whitney Houston and also your lovely voice. If you don't mind can you write back to me. I know that you don't have time but if you write back to me it will make me so happy so please write back to me. Good luck with your song career." From: Alex

"I luv the way Britney dances and sings. If there is anyone out there that reads this and hates Britney, e-mail me, we can have a little chat. Britney Spears ROCKS." From: cherie

"When I'm all grown up I want to be just like Brit. She's awesome!" From: Jessica

"Britney is so cool. I would give anything to go to a live concert and get backstage passes for my friend Whitney. [Hannah] Hi Britney! I'm your biggest fan! [So is Hannah] I would love to see you in person. I think it is really cool you met JC and Justin ['N Sync] at the Mickey Mouse Club." From: Hannah and Whitney

"Britney is really pretty. She has a beautiful voice and I would pay $500.00 or more to meet her. I'm a big fan. I see her on MTV all the time and I think, "Oh wow, she's great." I'm not gay, but she is beautiful and God really blessed her with her voice. Way to go Britany. Keep up the good work." From: Kristy

"Britney, you're number one in our hearts!!!!" From: Dari and Tears

"Britney you are so hot! Me and my friend think you are the coolest. I like all your photos and music. The CD was absolutely great! If you read this I hope you know our school, well at least all the guys anyway, think you are the best." From: Home boy

"Saying that a dream fulfilled is a dream shared, it is great to see a teen fulfill their dream, I believe Britney's rise to stardom is because of talent and great looks and dance moves. Go all the way Britney with full support from myself and those before and after me." From: Archimedean

"I've never met Britney in person (but I tell ya, I gotta be like her biggest fan alive), or have been to any of her concerts. It's because I live in Montreal (Quebec), she never really had an official concert here. There was a time when she was coming to the DOME, I had this great plan of how to skip school in the afternoon and go see her. To my surprise, which soon led to depression, she cancelled her tour in Montreal and went back Kentwood. The next day, the DJ (Rob Patrick) actually phoned her house and asked why she canned her tour in Montreal. She said she was too tired and sick of all this traveling. We faithful fans can all understand that. Britney Spears is the most beautiful and talented girl (and singer) I've ever

laid eyes on. I can't say that she's "hot," or that she's a good looking "chick," because I respect her with all my heart. Judging from what I heard from others, she must be a really nice, sweet, and kind person, with a warm golden heart. I wish her the best in her future for her evergrowing career."
From Rob.

"I am 14, and I love Britney Spears. I saw her in concert and it was fun until 'N Sync came on and none of the girls would stop screaming. Do you want to know why I am a big fan? I bought ten singles of her first single for all my friends for Christmas; One day I wore my school girl outfit with the feathers in my hair; I bought her CD the first day it came out; and I have a shrine of pictures. I think she is an awsome singer and my favorite song is "Crazy." Well gotta go to bed."
From: Vanessa

"Hey! My name is Hong and I'm from New Orleans (Metairie), Louisiana (Where Britney's from!!). I went the her concert on January 16, 1999 at the Centroplex Theater in Baton Rouge. She was wearing her glasses and a pink long sleeve shirt w/ blue jeans . . . she was soo cute!! She had her backpack on and she was carrying a bag. She waved and smiled and walked to the back entrance. I loved the concert. I wish she coulda performed the whole time instead of

'N Sync. I can't wait till she goes on tour by herself." From: Hong

"Britney, all I can say is that you are so hot. You make me watch your video all time. When I first saw you on television, everything got erased in my mind. What I was thinking was: What would I do to make this girl mine? Afterwards, I started thinking how completely "Sexy" you are!!! I love you girl!!! I wish you were mine!!!" From: Anthony

"North of Sweden is calling!! My name is Rickard. I am a professionell snowboard kid. I am 16 and very sweet and kind. It is true. But first of all I am a big Britney fan so I want to mail with her fans and if you, Britney read this, mail me." From: Rickard

"I really like you and your songs and you are so pretty to me and I wish I could meet you in person and go to your concerts and get an autograph from you. I am a big fan of yours and I would do anything for you. Be happy." From: Your fan, Teresa

"Britney Spears rules and anybody who doesn't like her is pretty stupid. Why do people waste their time making anti-Britney sites? Britney is very talented and beautiful. There should be at least 3,000 sites dedicated to how much we love her.'' From: Lilly

> Write to the star yourself at:
> Britney Fan Club
> PO BOX 7022
> Red Bank, New Jersey 07701-7022
>
> Or e-mail her at: britney@peeps.com

17

Wild Web Sites

Web sites have become the new libraries for many of us, and Britney's fans have done an amazing job keeping up on the newest Britney information and getting it out there for the world to see.

Sites come and go, but the nine here we hope will be around for a long, long time. They have an array of great facts, hard-to-find information, never-before-seen pictures, audio and video interviews, and memorabilia. The Web changes so frequently, they may work—or not. We've also supplied room for you to list your favorite spots.

1. *http://www.peeps.com/britney/index.html*

This is Britney's official Web site. Here you'll find information on everything about the star; bio, music, fan club, and backstage with Britney. Catch a glimpse of Britney when she was a little girl on *Star Search*, visit the Britney store, or download audio and video versions of exclusive interviews, like AOL's Entertainment Asylum. You'll hear and see real footage of the singer as she talks with Max Martin about her abilities, recording her first album, growing up performing, influences, studio performances, and her overseas experience. Since this is her official site, it's updated often and is a most reliable source.

2. *http://www.geocities.com/SunsetStrip/Cabaret/2955/index.html*

The Geocities site offer its viewers lots of diversity and by surfing under its name, you can find a ton of different pages—all which present Britney data. This specific site offers main info, total news updates, appearances, calendar, bio, picks, discography, multimedia, in print, fan club, awards, rings, chat room, message board, MMC, and guest book, plus a link to the Disney channel.

3. *http://reach.to/britney*

Self-proclaimed as "the most updated site" this one keeps its promise. Topics include appearances, news about Britney, multimedia, lyrics, look-alikes, club, chat, help Britney, transcripts, your turn, get in touch, and news articles. The best part by far is the never-before-seen pictures. See Britney sitting on Santa's lap, her first dance recital and her standing next to Mickey Mouse at

Disney World. There are also old article clippings from her pageant wins and *Star Search* appearances as well. And that's just the beginning. There's even a list of people who have impersonated Britney online. Just select a name and bingo, their e-mail address appears so you can give them a piece of your mind. The news is updated regularly, and it's international ranging from New York to Canada and everywhere else on the globe.

4. *http://www.multiboard.com/~spettit/mmc/index.html*

If you're a lover of Britney, 'N Sync, or the Mickey Mouse Club, you'll flip over this baby. Find individual pages for each cast member plus information on what they've done and where they are now. Features like request line, exclusives, fan feedback, bloopers, Q&A about the show, episode guides, songs and movies, most frequently asked questions plus their answers are just the tip of what you'll find. Get info on the original Mickey Mouse show, the Seventies remake, and of course, the New MMC. You can even talk to the site's creator, Sherri Pettit.

5. *http://www.ramstadt.com/britney/*

Called "The Britney Spears Links," this site is a great resource for any fan. It also connects you to many other interesting and riveting pages.

6. *http://starlight.virtualave.net/*

An awesome site dedicated to the new MMC, this page has stuff about 'N Sync, Britney, news, charts, articles, cover songs, awards, Web links . . . all sorts of cool stuff that lets you follow Britney's MMC years. JC, Justin, Keri, Christina, are included along with articles that have been written about the stars, Q&A with Britney and JC, hanging with MMC cast, and answered fan mail.

7. *http://www.justnikki.com/britney.html*

She was the cover queen for this hot, online magazine/catalogue, which offers its viewers fashion, accessories, interviews, and a Q&A with Britney.

8. *http://www.mtv.com/news/gallery/s/spears.html*

If you like MTV, you'll love this updated daily/ weekly site. Find out quick news flashes regarding Britney like shoots for fun, video debut, homecoming queen, interviews, *Dawson's Creek*, Spears with 'N Sync, life with 'N Sync, shooting her video, and her knee injury. And since each is categorized by date, it's totally easy to read and follow. Each update allows you to click on other related cites as well. For example, clicking onto ''Life with 'N Sync'' permits you to connect directly to 'N Sync updates, news-flashes, and more.

9. *http://www.billboard.com/*

For music lovers everywhere, this page lets you connect to the famous magazine while reading up-to-date news information. Weekly reports on various artists and groups along with what's going on in music industry. You can also get chart information on top songs, special reports, this week, and resources.

Didn't find your favorite site? Not to worry. Add your own hot Britney spots—this way, they're just a finger tip away.

1. Address:

Why it's good:

What makes it special:

2. Address:

Why it's good:

What makes it special:

3. Address:

Why it's good:

What makes it special:

4. Address:

Why it's good:

What makes it special:

5. Address:

Why it's good:

What makes it special:

6. Address:

Why it's good:

What makes it special:

7. Address:

Why it's good:

What makes it special:

8. Address:

Why it's good:

What makes it special:

9. Address:

Why it's good:

What makes it special:

10. Address:

Why it's good:

What makes it special:

18

Total Trivia

Just for Fun, Here's Some Good Ol' Fun Trivia Facts.

1. What nickname do Britney's friends call her?

2. Who is Britney's best friend?

3. What is Britney's favorite color?

4. What pets does Britney have? What are their names?

5. What gift does Britney want for Christmas?

6. What was Britney's 1999 New Year's Resolution?

7. What's Britney's fave food?

8. What famous actress did she work with in MMC?

9. What does Britney have a collection of and receive every Xmas?

10. At the American Music Awards, what musical group did Britney introduce?

11. What was the first song Britney recorded with Jive?

12. What does Britney love most about flying?

13. What part of traveling does Britney hate most?

14. Who plays the role of the teacher in the "...Baby One More Time" video?

15. Who is Britney's role model?

1. Britt
2. Her cousin Laura Lynn
3. Baby blue
4. Cain, Spotty, and Mom's dog, Sebastian.
5. Victoria's Secret bath stuff.
6. Stop biting her nails.
7. Cookie dough ice cream.
8. Keri Russell from *Felicity*.
9. Dolls
10. The Goo-Goo Dolls.
11. "From the Bottom of My Heart"
12. The plane food. "It's so cute and tiny."
13. Flying
14. Felicia, the woman who travels with Britney
15. Shania Twain

19

Time Line

December 2, 1981
Britney Jean Spears is born!

The early years 1982–1989
Britney plays the lead in school plays, shows her fancy footwork in dance recitals and wins several talent contests.

In 1990
Britney has her first audition for *The Mickey Mouse Club*. Though she doesn't get the gig, she does win the Miss Talent Central States Pageant in mid-August. She also makes an appearance on *Star Search*.

In 1991
While in New York, Britney shoots several commercials, plus she is cast in the Off-

Broadway production of *Ruthless*. Later on in the year she surfaces on *Star Search* again.

In 1992
April 23, Britney wins the Miss Talent USA pageant.

In 1993
A second audition for the MMC finally lands Britney a role. She stays for two seasons.

In 1995
MMC is canceled and Britney goes back to school. She spends the next year being really bored.

1996–1997
This is the year it all starts. Britney's dad sends a tape to Larry Rudolph, who becomes her manager. He in turn sends her tape to Jive Records. Britney and her mom fly to New York in the later part of the year. She meets with Jive who, after hearing her sing, sign her on the spot. Jive introduces her to Max and Eric, and at 15, Britney is set to record her first album.

Spring and Summer of 1998
Finishing touches are added to the record and the Jive promotion plan goes into action. Britney takes to the malls to perform her material.

Fall and Winter of 1998

Toward the end of October *Sabrina the Teenage Witch* album is released which includes "Soda Pop." In November, her single, ". . . Baby One More Time," is released and within weeks, makes its way up the chart. Britney joins the 'N Sync boys and their first concert performance is on the eighteenth. "Just Nikki" features the superstar on the cover of *Catalog*. In December, the *Sabrina* soundtrack goes gold, selling over 500,000 copies. *Billboard* magazine and *Bop* both have large articles on Britney.

January of 1999

The year starts off with a bang as Britney continues to tour with 'N Sync, making the last of the rounds by the seventh. Britney appears on *The Howie Mandel Show*, she is a presenter at the American Music Awards and by the twelfth, Britney's album is released. When the CD opens on the charts it's already at number one along with her single. ". . . Baby One More Time" hits Number 1 on hot 100 sales. On the eighteenth, reports come that ". . . Baby One More Time" has sold over 125,000 copies in its first week. On the twentieth she shoots Tommy Hilfiger's Spring ad. At the end of this month, *Billboard* reports Britney is the youngest debut female artist to have both a Number

1 single and album simultaneously. Both hit Number 1 on the top 100. Jonny Wright signs on as her manager.

February of 1999

Britney is on *The Rosie O'Donnell Show*, then later that day makes an appearance on *Total Request*. Britney signs with Company Modeling Agency and "... Baby One More Time" is released in the UK. Her pretty face can be seen in *People* magazine, *Girl's Life, Teen Celebrity*, and others. In mid-February Britney dislocates her knee and must cancel several special events, *The Tonight Show* and the Grammy Awards among them. To help soothe the pain of disappointment, MTV gives her a Grammy pajama party.

March 1999

Britney makes the magazine rounds and appears in *Newsweek, Time* and *Entertainment Weekly*. *Teen People* gives her a makeover, (ironically, in that same issue, her Tommy ad appears as well) and *Rolling Stone* visits her hometown for a major photo shoot. Britney is supposed to appear on MTV's *Spring Break* in Cancun, Mexico but because of her knee surgery, she pre-tapes the segment instead. Her album is released in Japan.

About the Author

Alix Strauss is a freelance writer living in New York City. A graduate of New York University, she has published articles in many magazines and newspapers, including *The New York Times, Seventeen, Twist, React, Family Circle, Maxim,* and *Marie Claire.* Presently, she divides her time between writing, producing, and teaching.